The Complete Keyboard Player
Book 3

SONGS

Angels	24
Can't Get You Out Of My Head	8
Clocks	44
Don't Cry For Me Argentina	41
(Everything I Do) I Do It For You	30
Hava Nagila	34
I'll Be There For You (Theme From *Friends*)	38
I'm A Believer	16
In The Air Tonight	33
Isn't She Lovely	29
Livin' La Vida Loca	37
Mamma Mia	42
Ob-La-Di, Ob-La-Da	14
Reach	18
She's The One	22
Space Oddity	10
Star Wars (Main Theme)	46
The Winner Takes It All	4
When I'm Sixty Four	26
Yesterday	6

About This Book	3

LESSONS

1	Chord of E7	4
2	Chord of E Minor: Em	8
3	Scale of C - Key of C; Scale of F - Key of F	12
	Chord of B♭; Chord of F7	13
4	Triplets, Sixteenth Notes (Semiquavers), and Dotted Rhythms	20
5	Scale of G - Key of G	24
6	Chords of G Minor: Gm and B♭ Minor: B♭m	28
7	Minor Keys; Key of D Minor	32
8	Key of E Minor; Chord of B Minor: Bm	36
9	Key of B Flat, Chord of E♭	40
10	Chord of C Minor: Cm	44
	Chord Chart	48

Published by:
Hal Leonard

Exclusive Distributors:
Hal Leonard
7777 West Bluemound Road,
Milwaukee, WI 53213
Email: info@halleonard.com

Hal Leonard Europe Limited
1 Red Place
London, W1K 6PL
Email: info@halleonardeurope.com

Hal Leonard Australia Pty. Ltd.
4 Lentara Court, Cheltenham,
Victoria 9132, Australia
Email: info@halleonard.com.au

This book © Copyright 2003 by Wise Publications

For all works contained herein:
Unauthorized copying, arranging, adapting, recording, Internet posting, public performance, or other distribution of the music in this publication is an infringement of copyright.
Infringers are liable under the law.

Written and arranged by Kenneth Baker.
Music processed by Paul Ewers Music Design.
Edited by Sorcha Armstrong.

Cover & book design by Chloë Alexander Design.
Artist photographs courtesy of
London Features International and Redferns.

CD recorded, mixed and mastered by Paul Honey.

Printed in the UK

www.halleonard.com

About This Book

IN BOOK 3 of *The Complete Keyboard Player* you learn about scales and keys. When you play in different keys you make basic changes of sound, and so add a new dimension to your playing. Minor keys, especially, can change the whole flavour of your music. In Book 3 you play in five new keys, including two minor keys.

In Book 3 you continue your left hand studies, with the emphasis as usual on 'fingered' chords. Ten new chords are introduced, in easy stages; at this level, the chord shapes no longer appear at the beginning of each song but if you get stuck, turn to the Chord Chart on page 48.

There is plenty for your right hand in Book 3. There are double notes, chords, fill-ins and counter-melodies. You will also learn more notes.

As usual, throughout the book you will get tips on how to use the facilities of the keyboard – the sounds, the rhythms and so on – more effectively.

Although Book 3 continues in the 'teach yourself' tradition of the earlier books, all teachers of the instrument will want to make it one of their standard text books.

If you have purchased the CD edition, all the songs in the book are featured on a high-quality CD, played with a full-band accompaniment, which will help you learn even faster!

Lesson 1

Chord of E7

USING SINGLE-FINGER CHORD method:
Locate **E** in the accompaniment section of your keyboard.
Convert this note into **E**7 (see Book 1, p42 and your owner's manual).

FINGERED CHORDS: ON

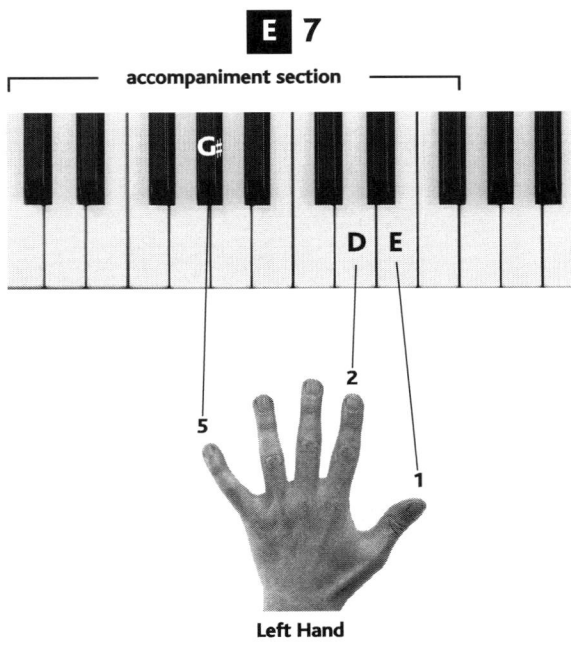

Left Hand

The Winner Takes It All

Words & Music by Benny Andersson & Björn Ulvaeus

Abba

Voice: **piano**
Rhythm: **rock**
Tempo: **medium** (♩ = 120)
Synchro-start: **on**

VERSE

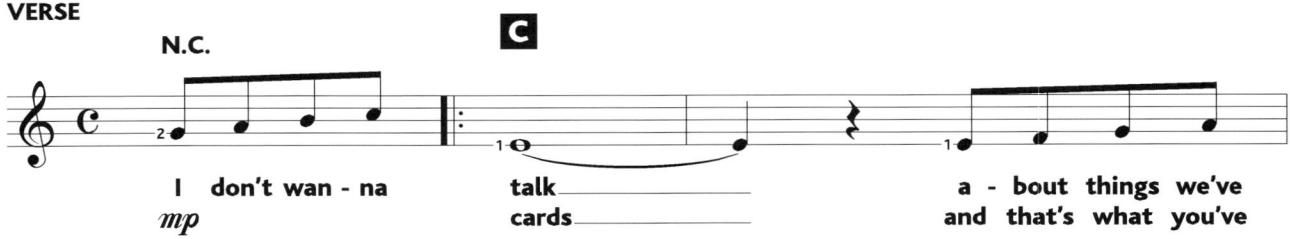

I don't wan-na talk   a - bout things we've
                cards   and that's what you've

gone   through   though it's hurt-ing   me
done   too   no - thing more to   say

© Copyright 1980 Union Songs AB, Stockholm, Sweden for the world.
Bocu Music Limited for Great Britain and the Republic of Ireland. All Rights Reserved. International Copyright Secured.

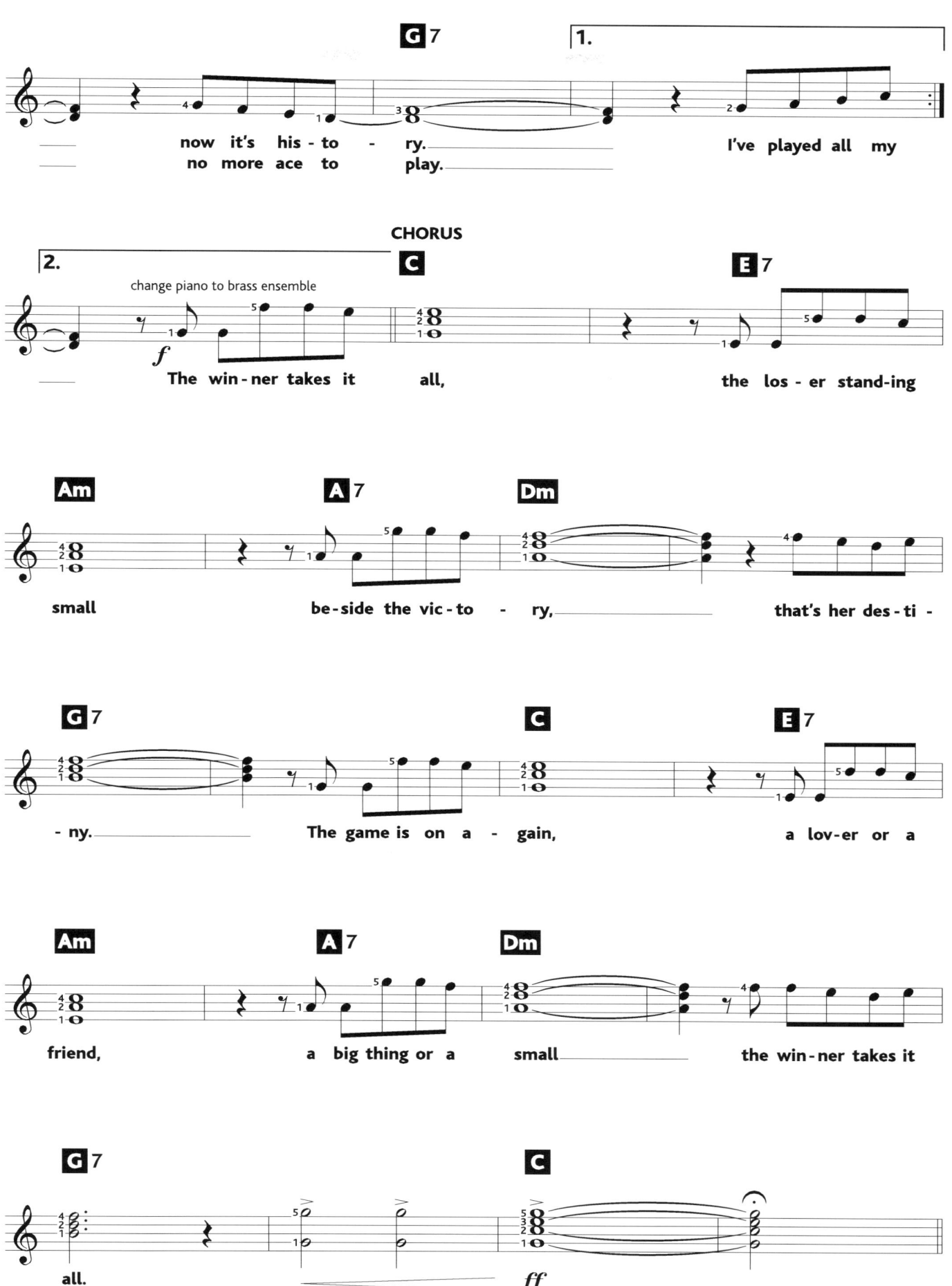

Yesterday

Words & Music by John Lennon & Paul McCartney

The Beatles

Voice: **piano**
Rhythm: **8 beat rock**
Tempo: **medium** (♩= 92)
Synchro-start: **on**

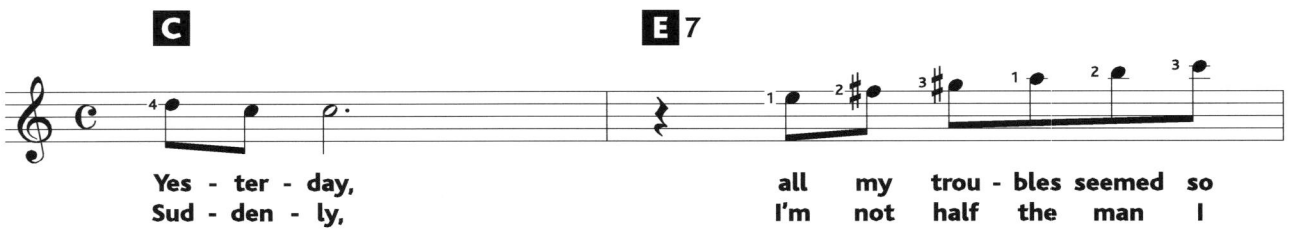

Yes - ter - day,   all my trou - bles seemed so
Sud - den - ly,   I'm not half the man I

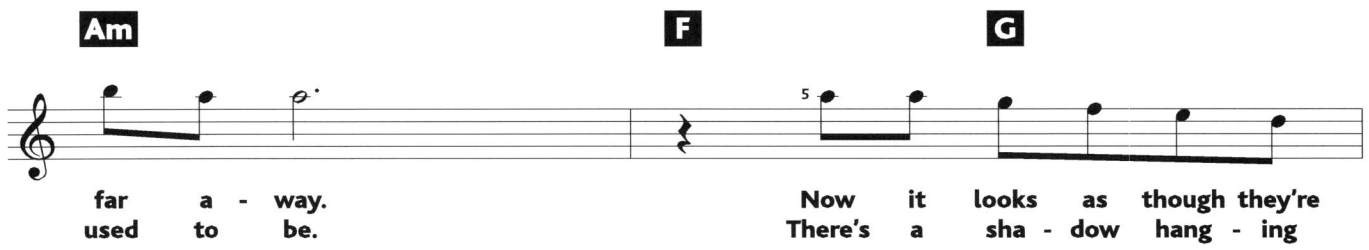

far a - way.   Now it looks as though they're
used to be.   There's a sha - dow hang - ing

here to stay. Oh, I be - lieve in
ov - er me. Oh, yes - ter - day came

yes - ter - day.   Why she had to go I don't
sud - den - ly.

know, she would - n't say.   I said

© Copyright 1965 Northern Songs.
All Rights Reserved. International Copyright Secured.

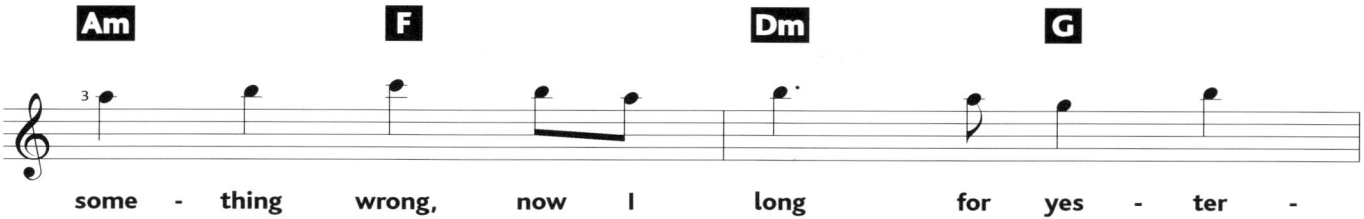
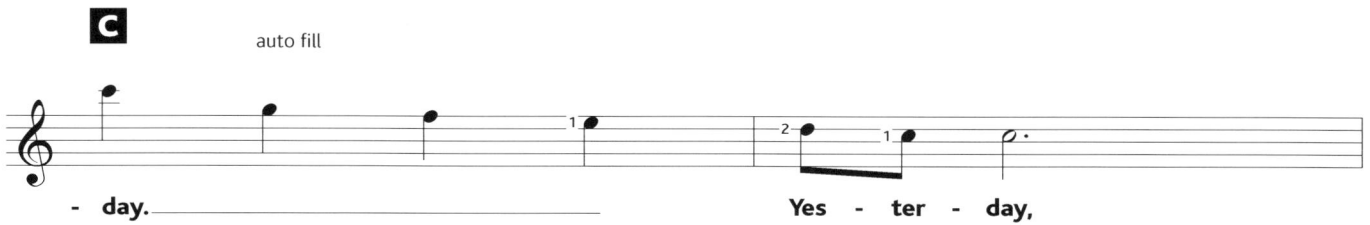
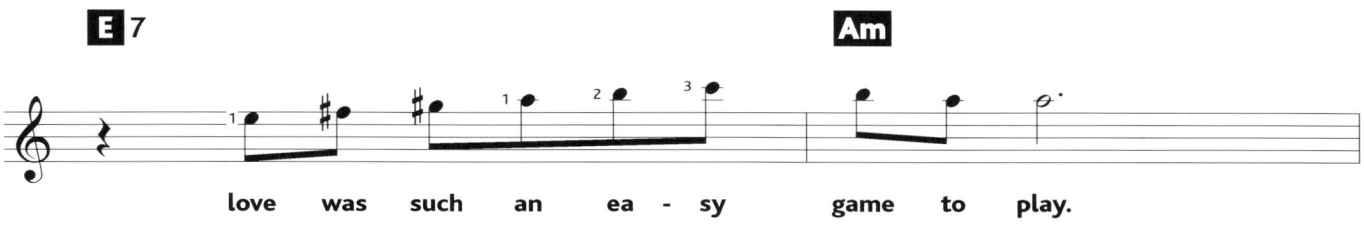
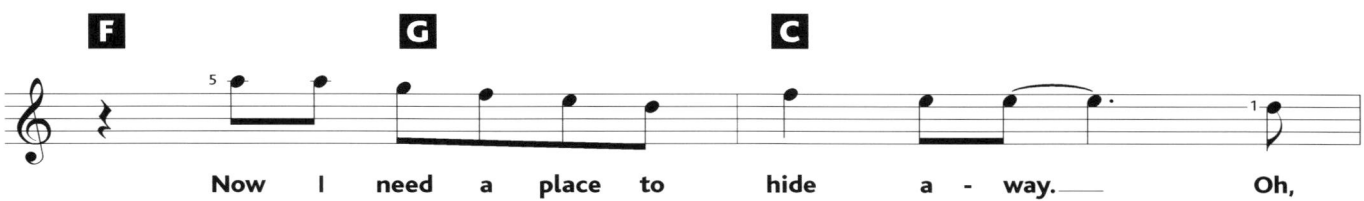
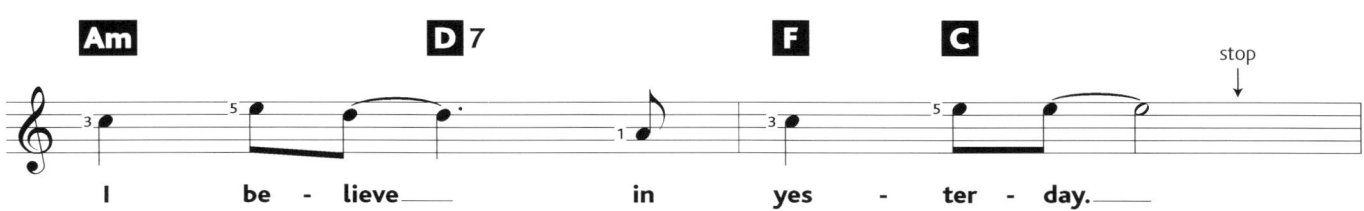

Freely

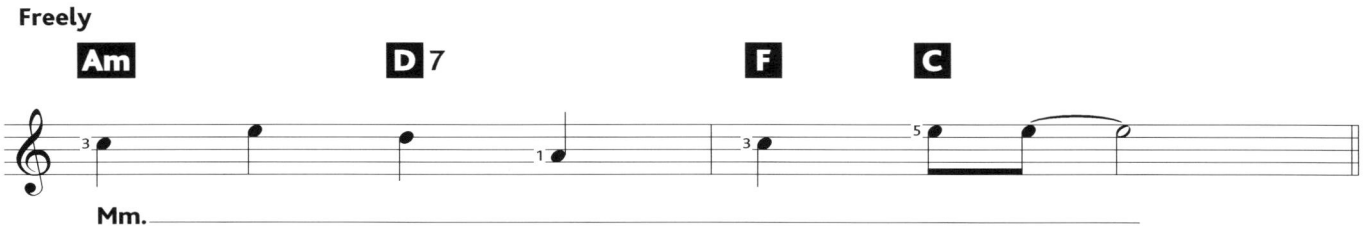

Chord of E Minor Em

Using single-finger chord method:

Locate **E** in the accompaniment section of your keyboard. Convert this note into **Em**

(see Book 2, page 30 and your owner's manual).

Using fingered chord method

See diagram (right).

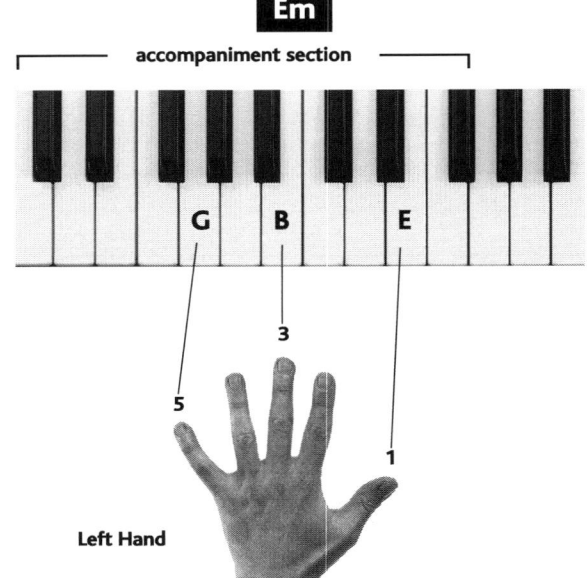

Can't Get You Out Of My Head

Words & Music by Cathy Dennis & Rob Davis

Kylie Minogue

Voice: **organ**
Rhythm: **disco**
Tempo: **medium** (♩ = 126)

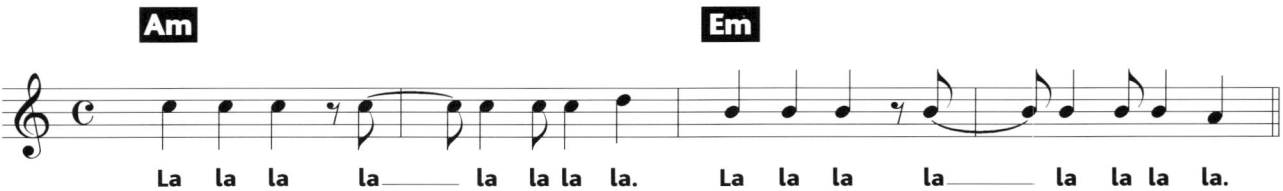

La la la la la la la la. La la la la la la la la.

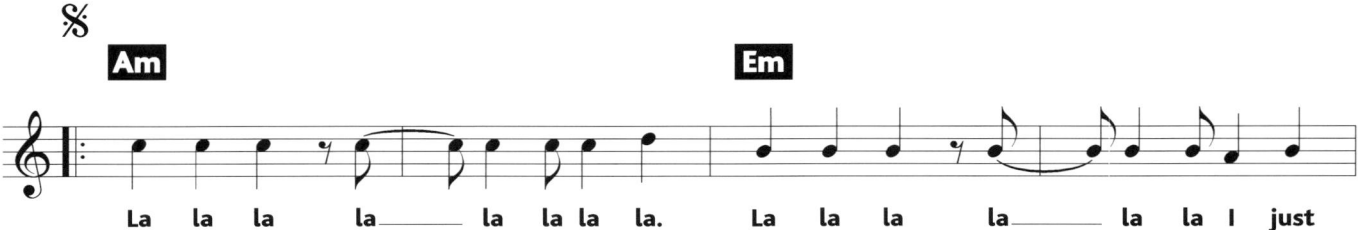

La la la la la la la. La la la la la la I just

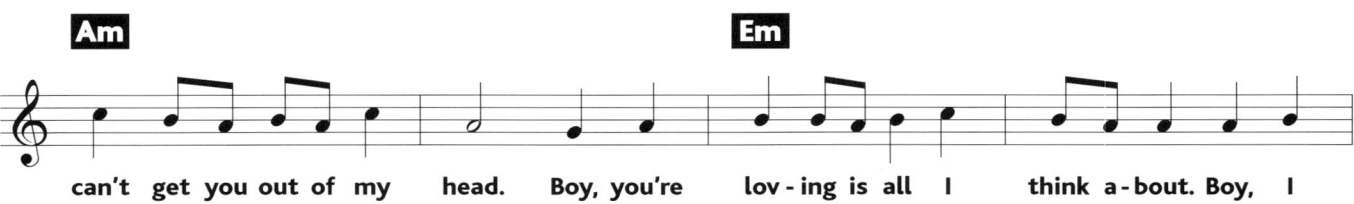

can't get you out of my head. Boy, you're lov-ing is all I think a-bout. Boy, I

© Copyright 2001 EMI Music Publishing Limited (50%)/Universal/MCA Music Limited (50%).
All Rights Reserved. International Copyright Secured.

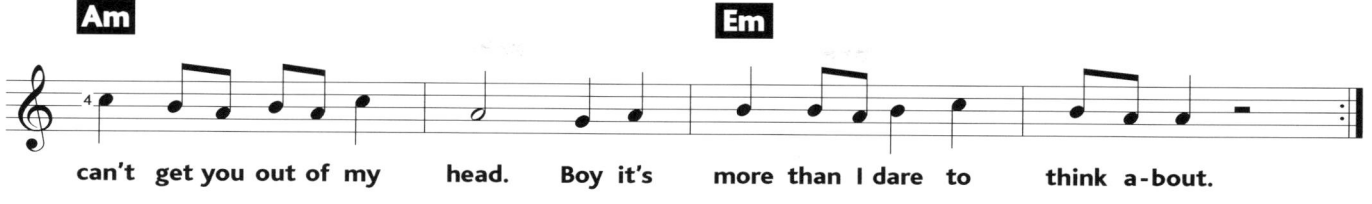
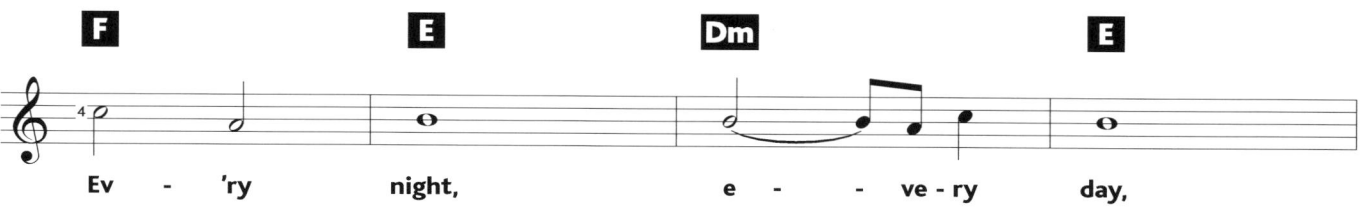
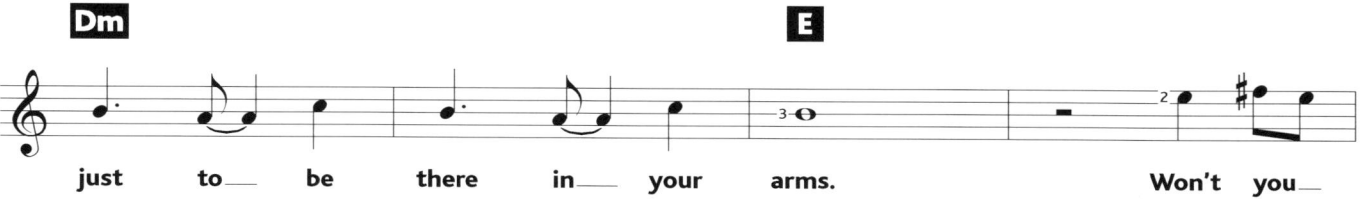
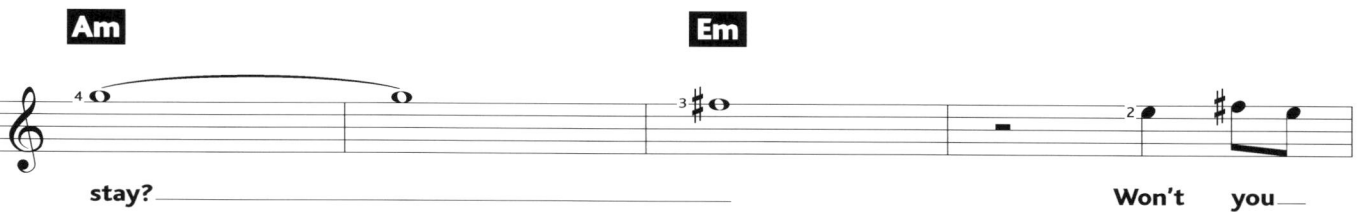
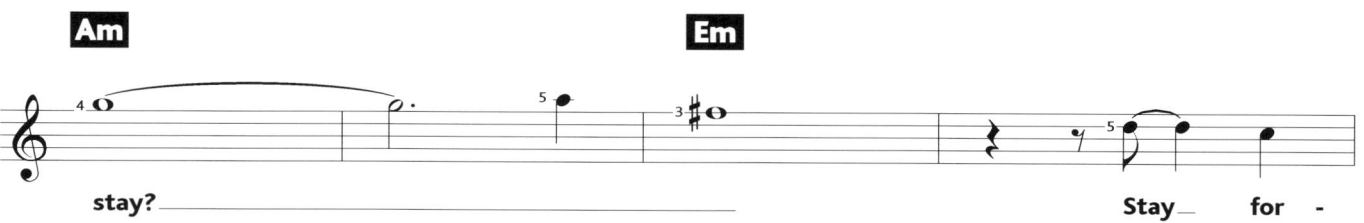
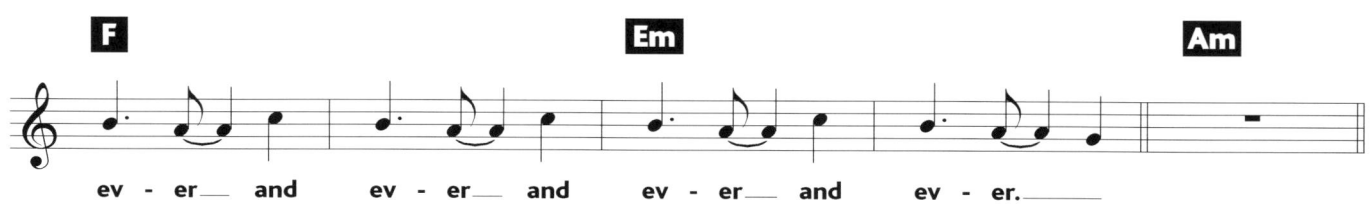

David Bowie

Space Oddity

Words & Music by David Bowie

Voice: **distorted guitar**
Rhythm: **rock ballad**
Tempo: **fast** (♩ = 135)
Synchro-start: **on**

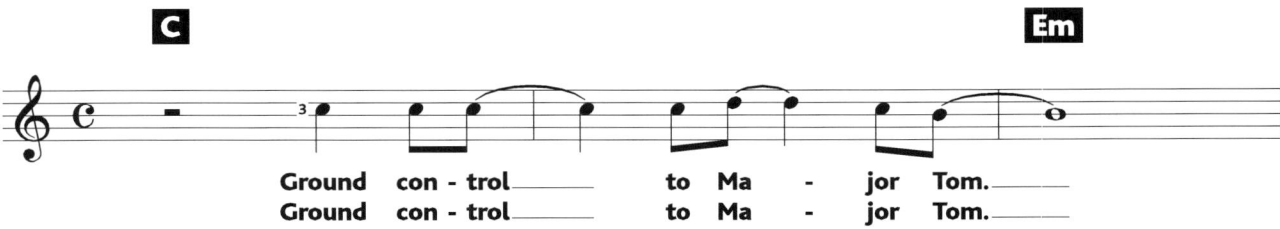
Ground con-trol to Ma-jor Tom.
Ground con-trol to Ma-jor Tom.

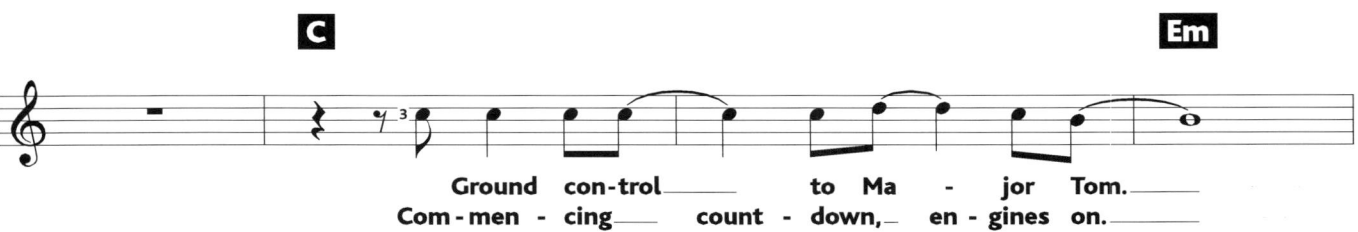
Ground con-trol to Ma-jor Tom.
Com-men-cing count-down, en-gines on.

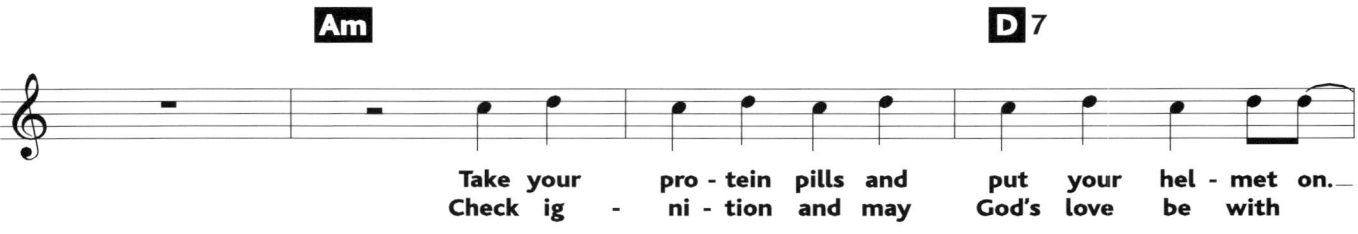
Take your pro-tein pills and put your hel-met on.
Check ig-ni-tion and may God's love be with

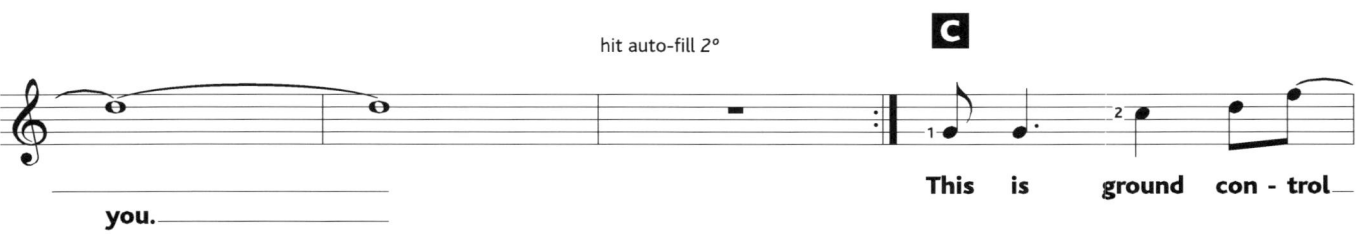
you.
This is ground con-trol

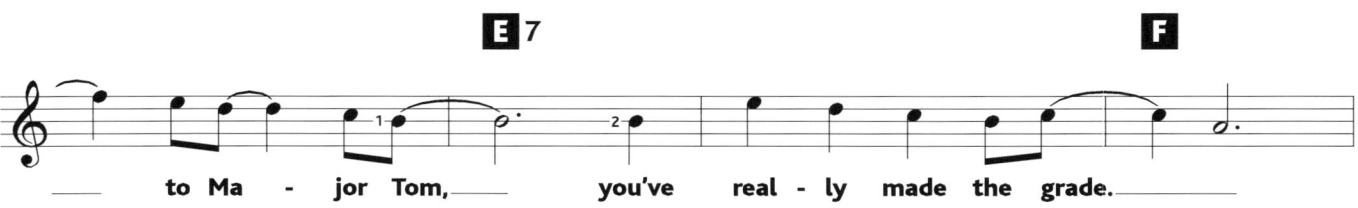
to Ma-jor Tom, you've real-ly made the grade.

© Copyright 1969 Onward Music Limited.
All Rights Reserved. International Copyright Secured.

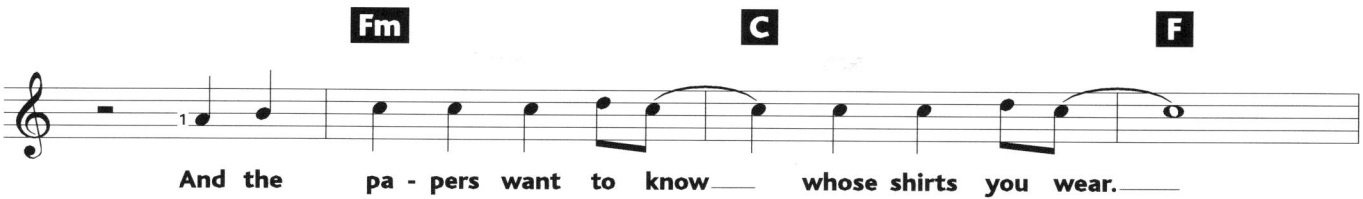
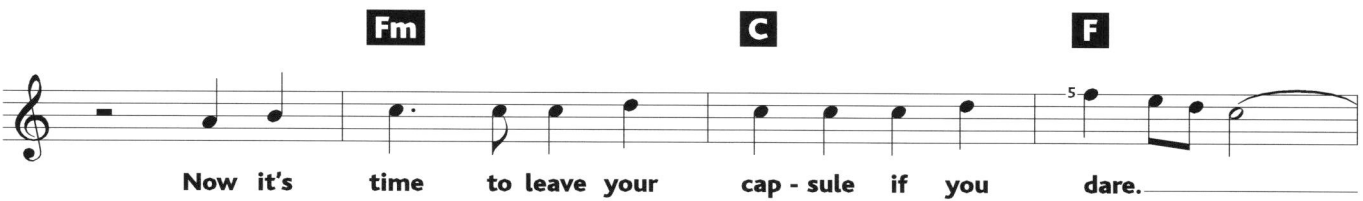
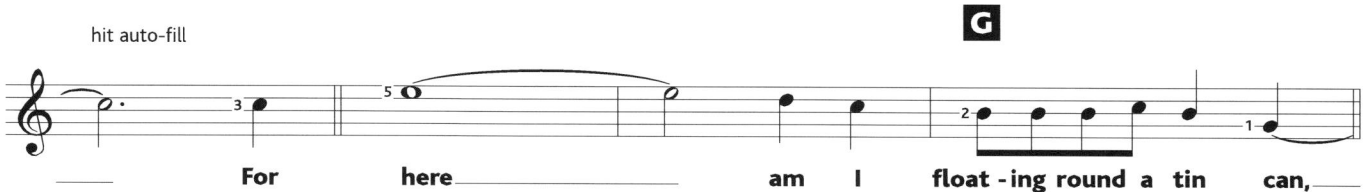
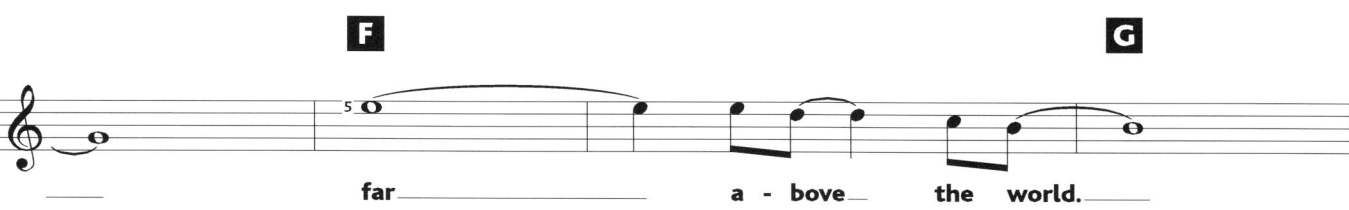
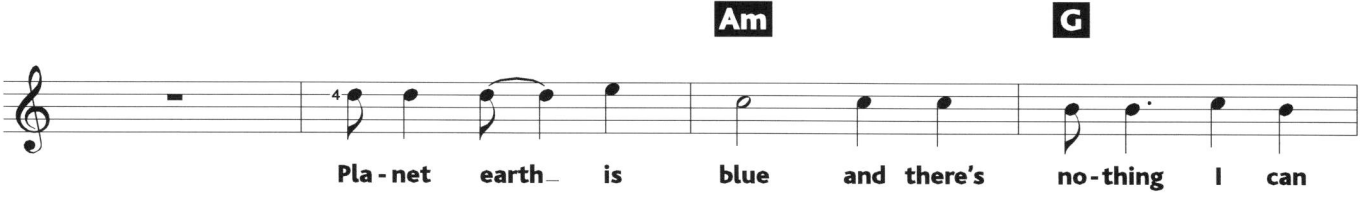
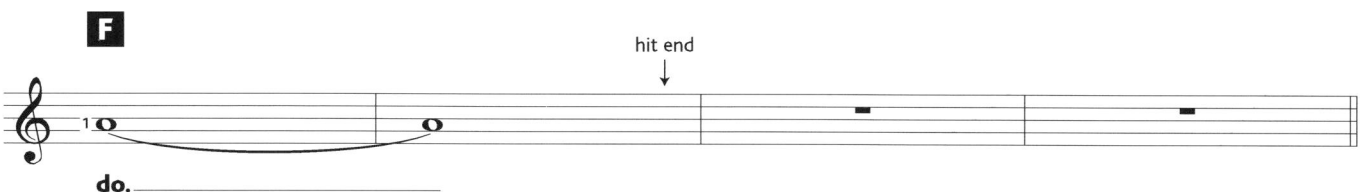

Scale of C - Key of C

A SCALE IS A succession of adjoining notes:

Scale of C (major)

As you see, there are no black notes in the scale of C.

When a piece is built on this scale, it is said to be in the '**key of C**'.
Almost all the pieces you have played so far have been in the key of C.

The occasional black notes you encountered in those pieces were of a temporary nature only, and did not affect the overall key.

From now on you are going to play in a number of different keys.

Scale of F - Key of F

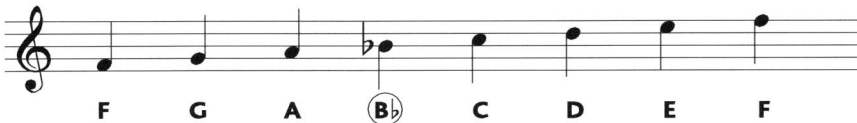

Scale of F (major)

As you can see, a B flat is required to form the scale of F.

When you are playing in this key, therefore, you must remember to play all your B's, wherever they might fall on the keyboard, as B flats.

To remind you, a B flat is inserted at the beginning of every line:

key signature

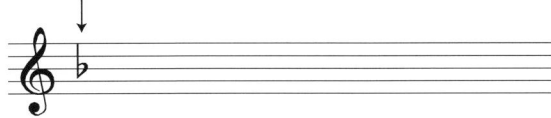

Look out for B flats at the beginning of the lines in the following songs.

Chord of B♭

YOU NEED THESE two chords in order to play the next songs.

Using single-finger chord method:

Locate 'B♭' in the accompaniment section of your keyboard. Play this note on its own and you will have a chord of B♭ major. To find B♭, look to the black note directly to the left of C.

Using fingered chord method:

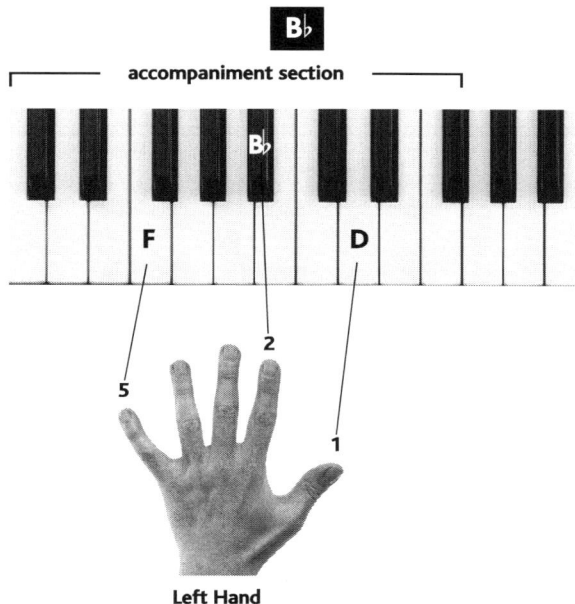

Left Hand

Chord of F7

Using single-finger chord method:

Locate '**F**' in the accompaniment section of your keyboard. Convert this into F 7 (see Book 1, page 42 and your owner's manual). To find F, look to the white note directly to the left of the group of 3 black notes.

Using fingered chord method:

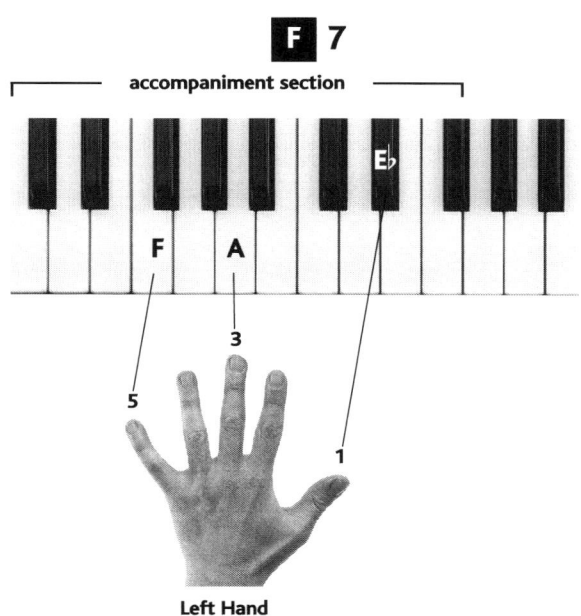

Left Hand

Ob-La-Di, Ob-La-Da

Words & Music by John Lennon & Paul McCartney

Paul McCartney

Voice: **piano**
Rhythm: **swing**
Tempo: **medium** (♩ = 118)
Synchro-start: **on**

VERSE

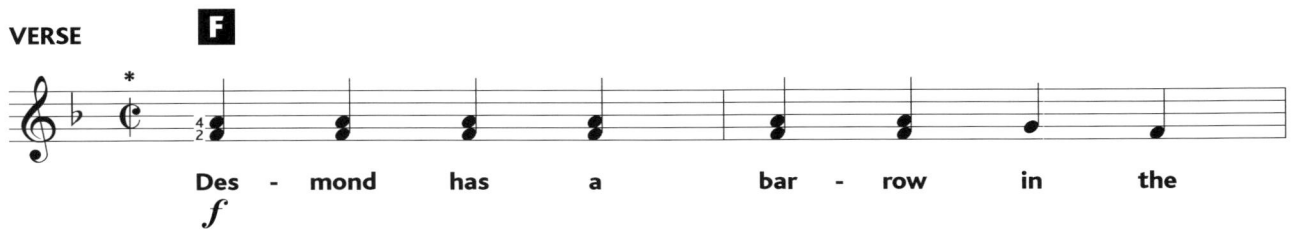

Des - mond has a bar - row in the

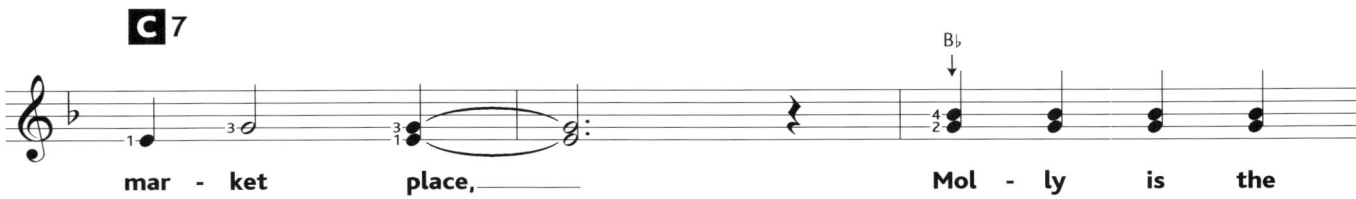

mar - ket place, Mol - ly is the

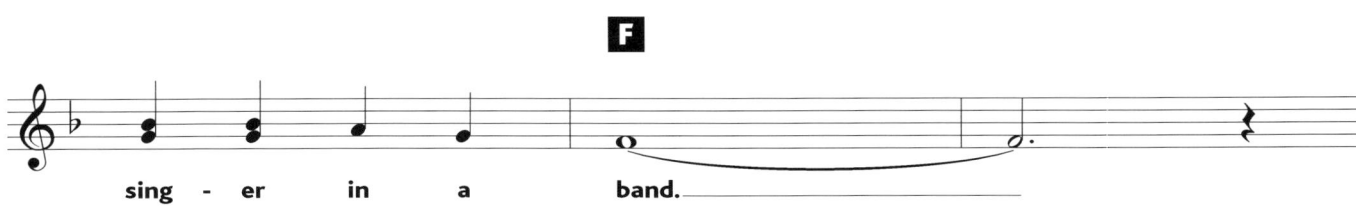

sing - er in a band.

Des - mond says to Mol - ly, girl, I like your face

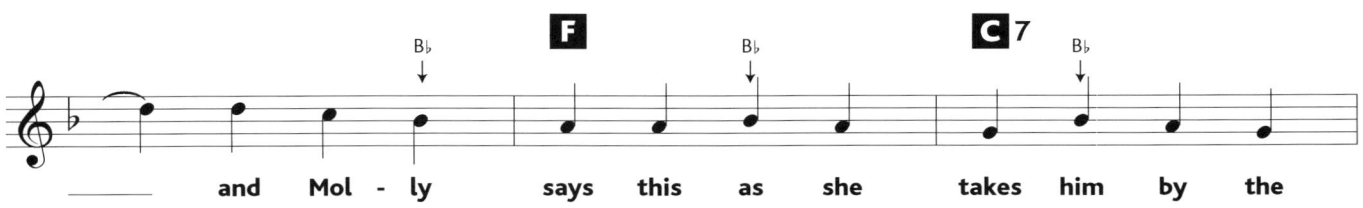

and Mol - ly says this as she takes him by the

© Copyright 1968 Northern Songs.
All Rights Reserved. International Copyright Secured.

*2/2 or 'cut' time: each bar has 2 half-note (minim) beats.

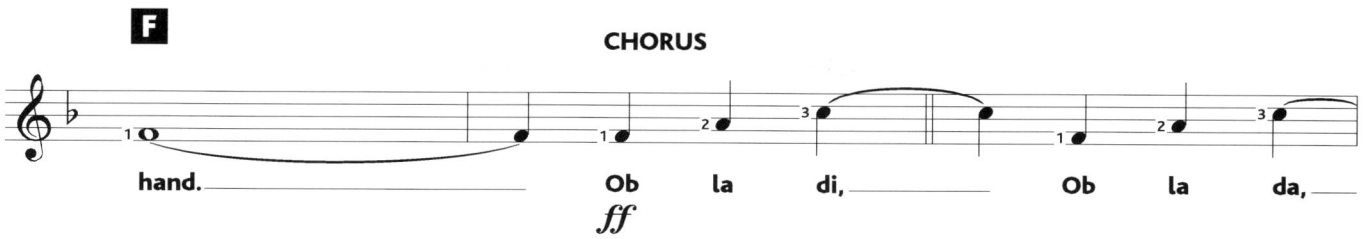
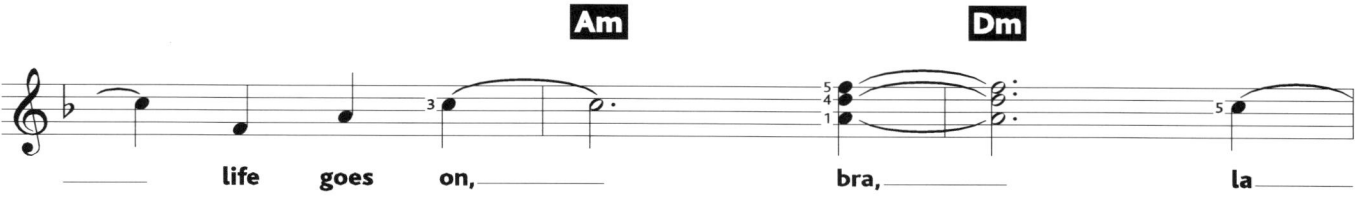
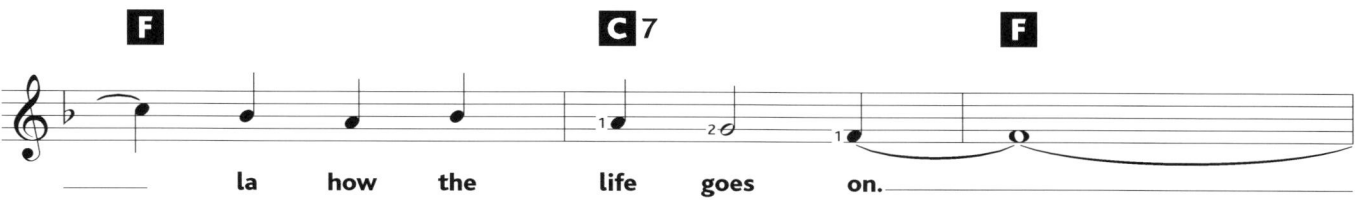
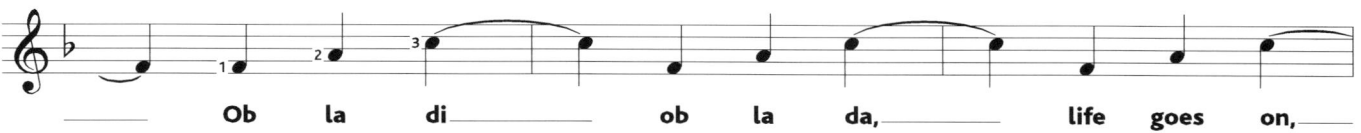
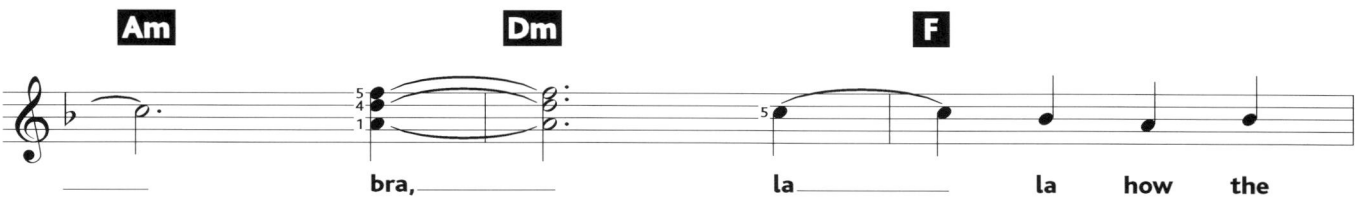
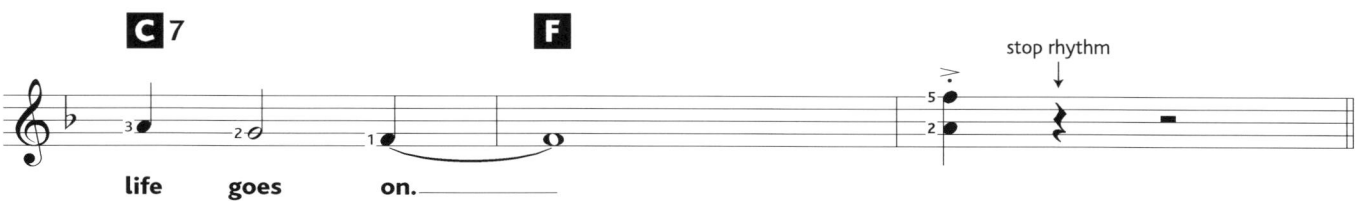

The Monkees

I'm A Believer

Words & Music by Neil Diamond

Voice: **organ**
Rhythm: **8-beat rock 'n' roll**
Tempo: **fast** (♩ = 160)

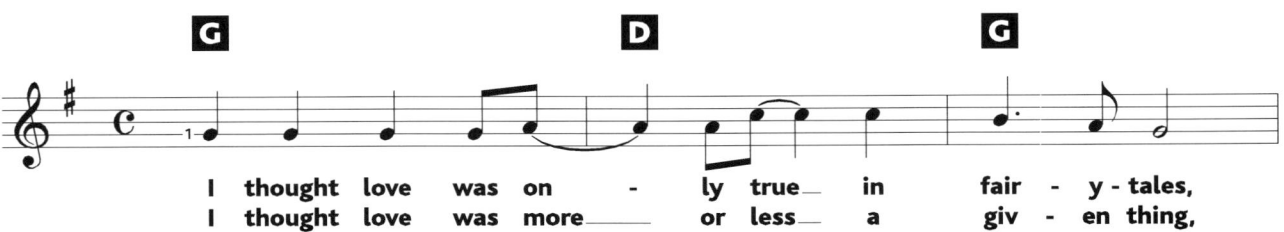

I thought love was on - ly true in fair - y - tales,
I thought love was more or less a giv - en thing,

meant for some - one else, but not for me.
seems the more I gave, the less I got.

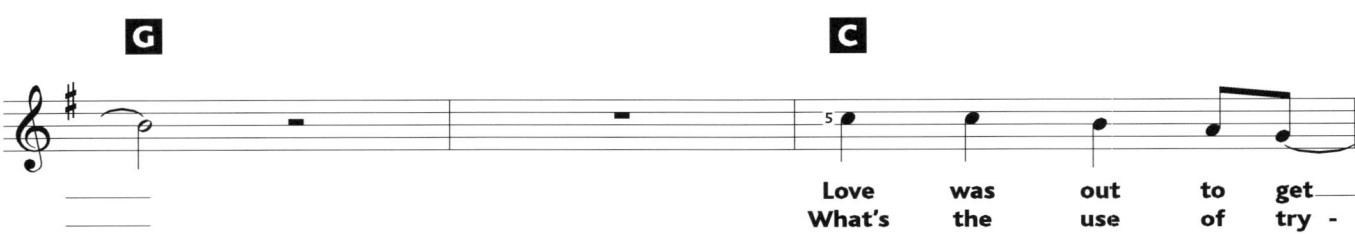

Love was out to get
What's the use of try -

me, that's the way it seemed.
- in'? All you get is pain.

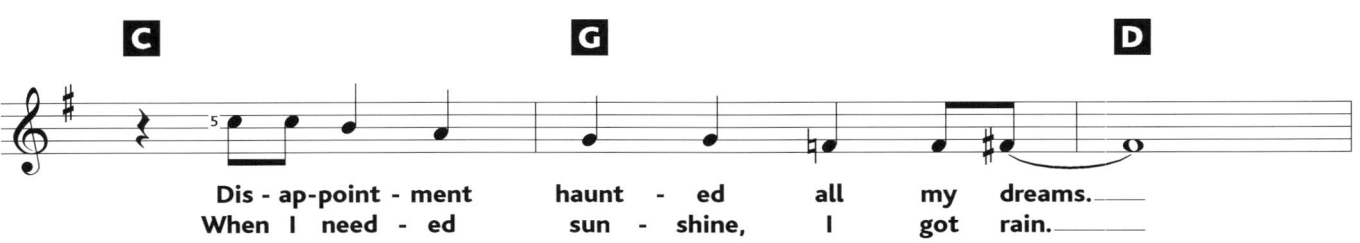

Dis - ap - point - ment haunt - ed all my dreams.
When I need - ed sun - shine, I got rain.

© Copyright 1966 Stonebridge Music Incorporated/Colgems-EMI Music Incorporated, USA.
Sony/ATV Music Publishing (UK) Limited (75%)/Screen Gems-EMI Music Limited (25%). All Rights Reserved. International Copyright Secured.

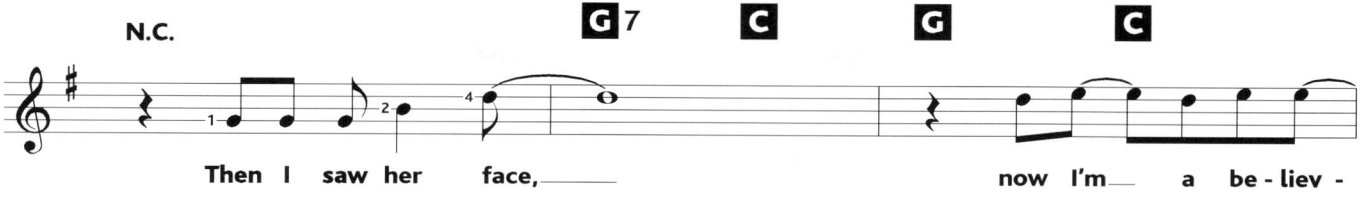
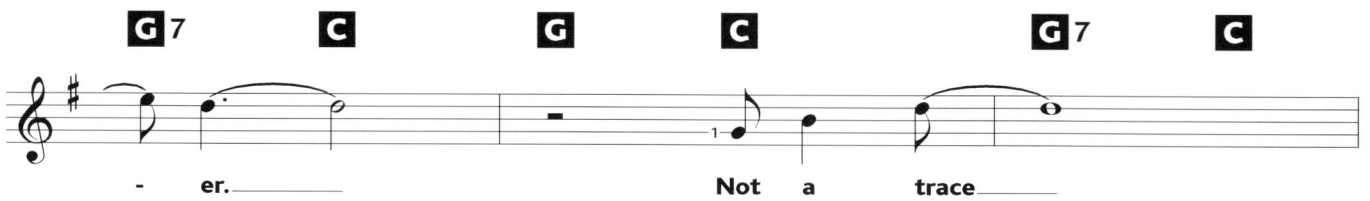

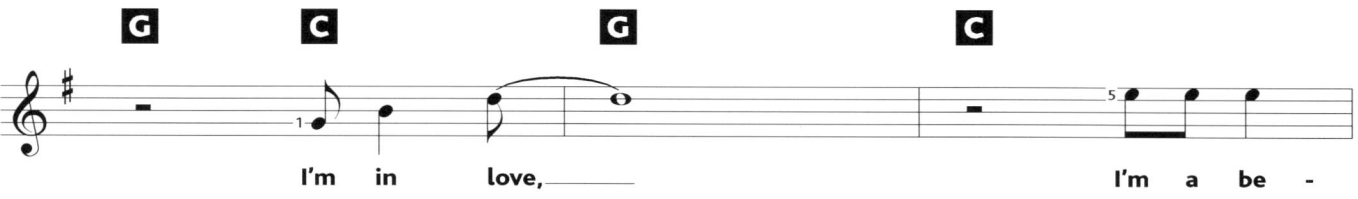

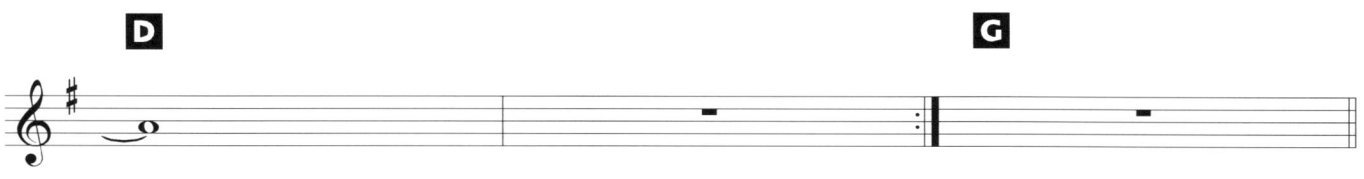

S Club 7

Reach

Words & Music by Cathy Dennis & Andrew Todd

Voice: **saxophone**
Rhythm: **rock shuffle**
Tempo: **fast** (♩=167)

When the world leaves you feel-ing blue, you can

count on me, I will be there for you.

When it seems all your hopes and dreams are a mil-lion

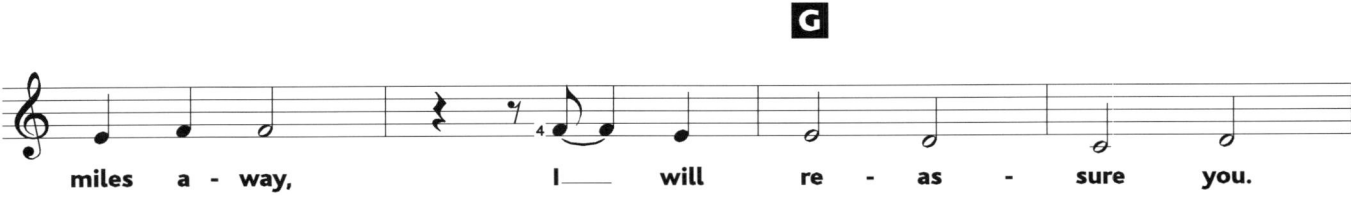

miles a-way, I will re-as-sure you.

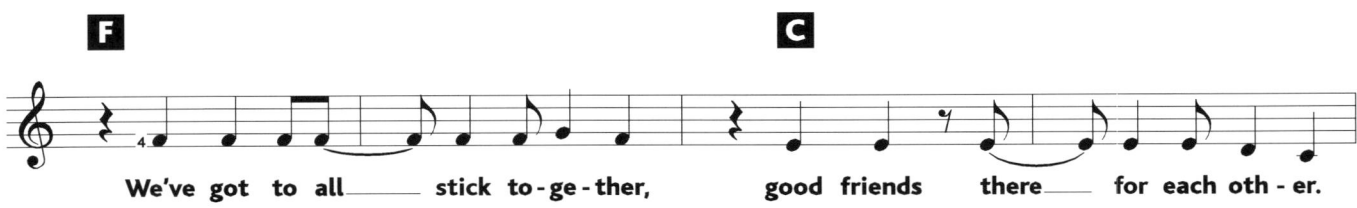

We've got to all stick to-ge-ther, good friends there for each oth-er.

© Copyright 2000 EMI Music Publishing Limited (50%)/BMG Music Publishing Limited (50%).
All Rights Reserved. International Copyright Secured.

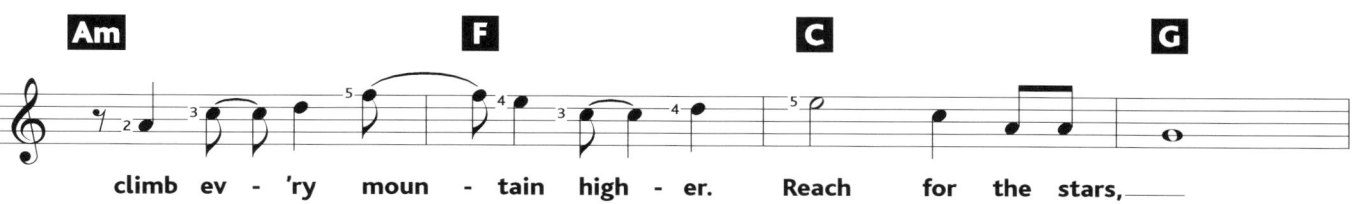

Triplets

A **TRIPLET** IS A group of three notes played in the time of two:

Eighth note (quaver) triplets must be played slightly faster than normal eighth notes, in order to fit them to the beat.

Compare the following two examples:

normal eighth notes (quavers)

count: 1   and   2   and   3   and   4   and

If you incorporate the word 'triplet' into your counting like this, you will get the feeling of the triplets.

normal eighth notes (quavers)

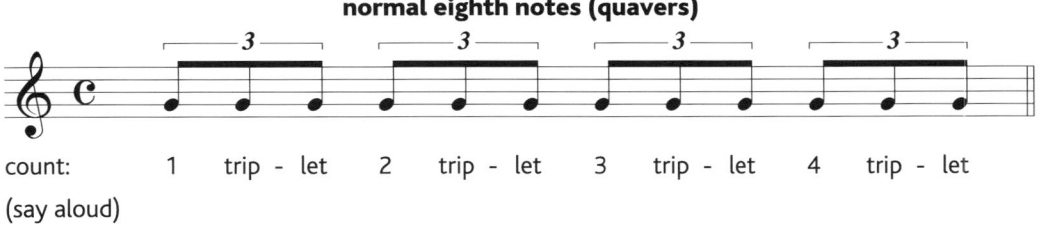

count: 1   trip - let   2   trip - let   3   trip - let   4   trip - let
(say aloud)

Sixteenth Notes (Semiquavers) and Dotted Rhythms

AN EIGHTH NOTE (QUAVER) can be subdivided into two sixteenth notes (semiquavers):

A 'dotted' eighth note is equal to half as much again (see 'dotted notes' in Book 2), that is, three sixteenth notes:

dotted eighth note · · · sixteenth notes

In practice, a dotted eighth note usually pairs up with a sixteenth note:

dotted eighth note · · · sixteenth note

Together these two notes are equivalent to four sixteenth notes, or one quarter note (crotchet):

3 sixteenth + 1 sixteenth = quarter
notes   note   note

The general effect of a passage like this:

is of eighth notes (quavers) with a 'lilt'.

The phrase 'humpty-dumpty' can be used as a guide to this rhythm:

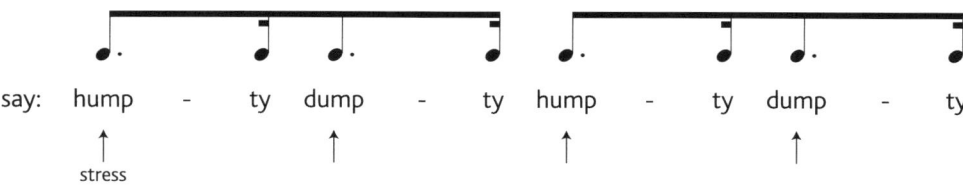

say: hump - ty dump - ty hump - ty dump - ty
     ↑   ↑   ↑   ↑
     stress

These uneven types of rhythms are often called 'dotted rhythms'. Look out for dotted rhythms in the next pieces.

She's The One

Words & Music by Karl Wallinger

Robbie Williams

Voice: **piano**
Rhythm: **slow rock**
Tempo: **slow** (♩ = 78)

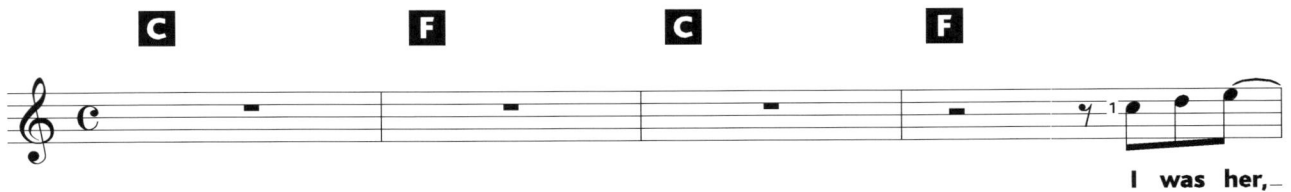

I was her,

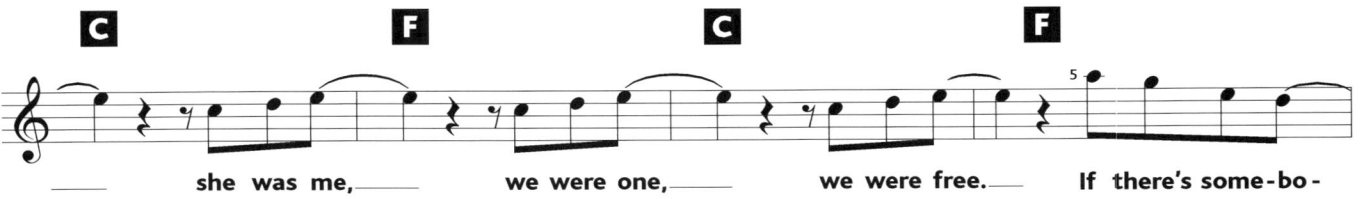

she was me, we were one, we were free. If there's some-bo-

-dy call-ing me on, she's the one. If there's some-bo-

-dy call-ing me on, she's the one. We were young,

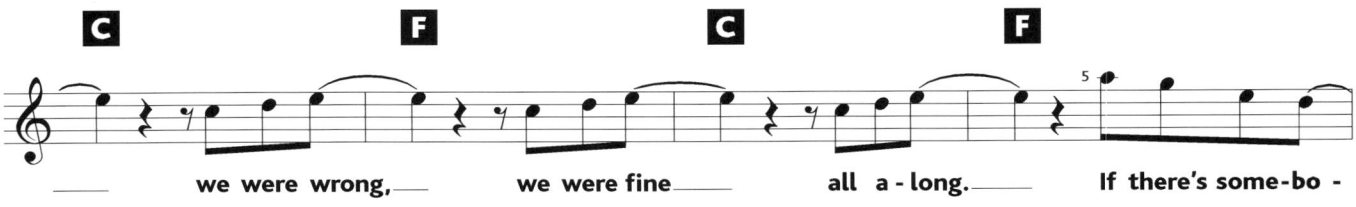

we were wrong, we were fine all a-long. If there's some-bo-

© Copyright 1996 PolyGram Music Publishing Limited.
Universal Music Publishing Limited. All Rights Reserved. International Copyright Secured.

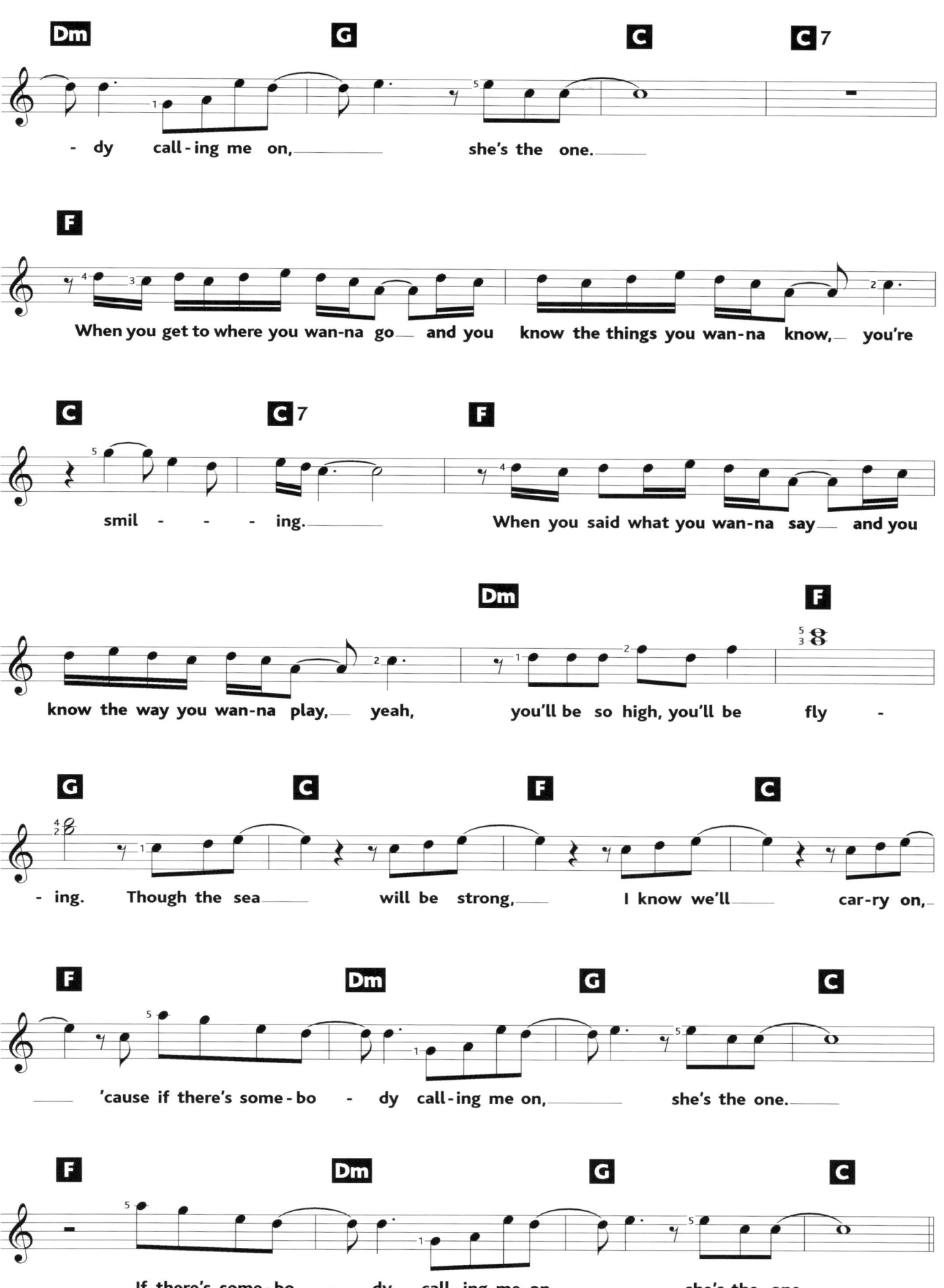

Scale of G - Key of G

AN F SHARP is required to form the scale of G.

When a piece is built on this scale it is said to be 'in the key of G'. When you are playing in this key you must remember to play all F's, wherever they might fall on the keyboard, as F sharps. The key signature, which appears at the beginning of every line, will remind you:

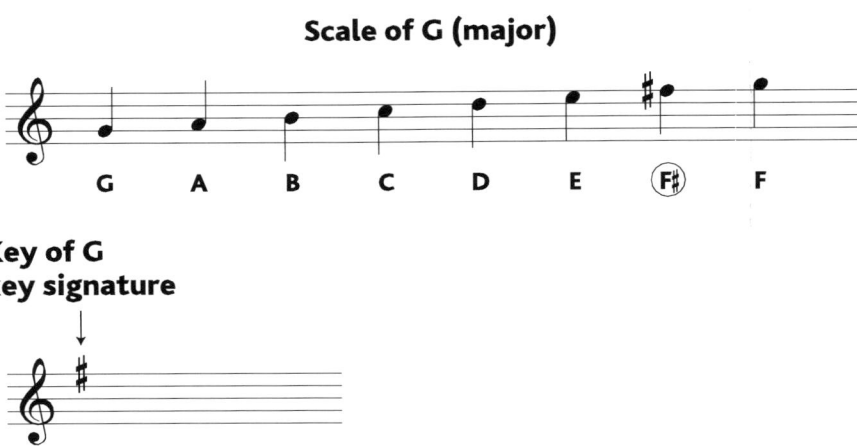

Angels

Words & Music by Robbie Williams & Guy Chambers

Robbie Williams

Voice: **piano**
Rhythm: **slow rock**
Tempo: **slow** (♩ = 72)
Synchro-start: **on**

I sit and wait. Does an an - gel con - tem - plate my fate?

And do they know the pla - ces where we go when we're grey and old?

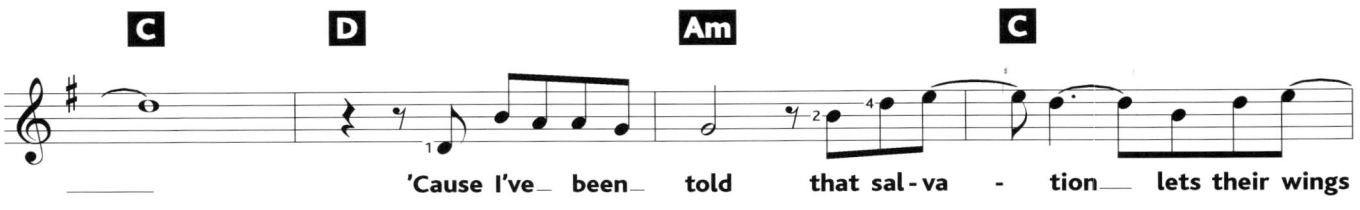

'Cause I've been told that sal - va - tion lets their wings

© Copyright 1997 EMI Virgin Music Limited (50%)/BMG Music Publishing Limited (50%).
All Rights Reserved. International Copyright Secured.

When I'm Sixty Four

Words & Music by John Lennon & Paul McCartney

Paul McCartney

Voice: **clarinet**
Rhythm: **swing**
Tempo: **medium** (♩ = 125)
Synchro-start: **on**

When I get old-er, los-ing my hair, ma-ny years from

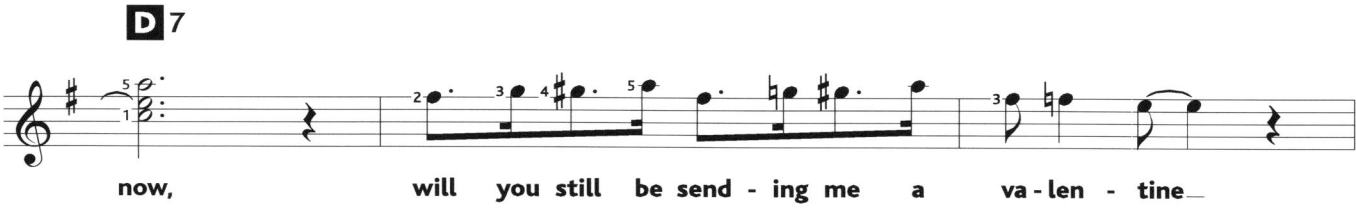
now, will you still be send-ing me a va-len-tine

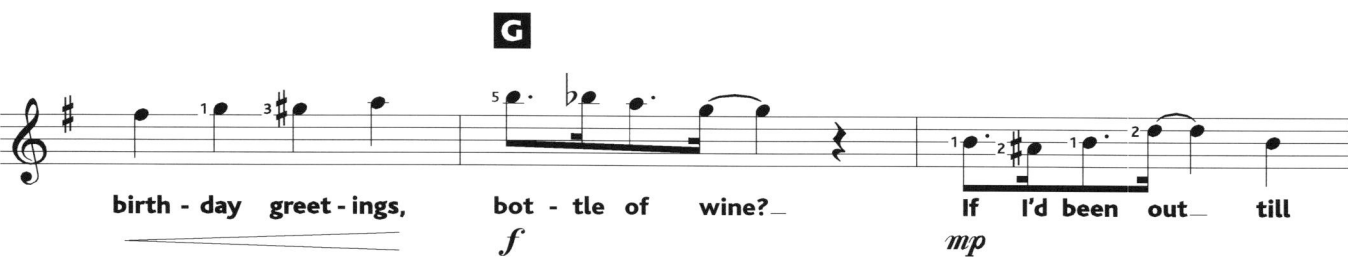
birth-day greet-ings, bot-tle of wine? If I'd been out till

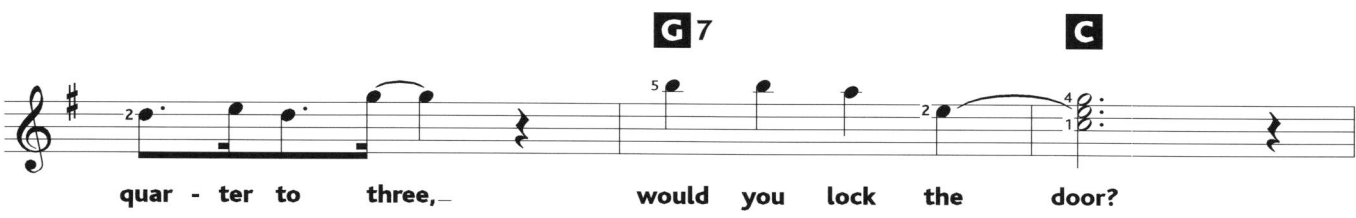
quar-ter to three, would you lock the door?

Will you still need me, will you still feed me, when I'm six-ty

© Copyright 1967 Northern Songs.
All Rights Reserved. International Copyright Secured.

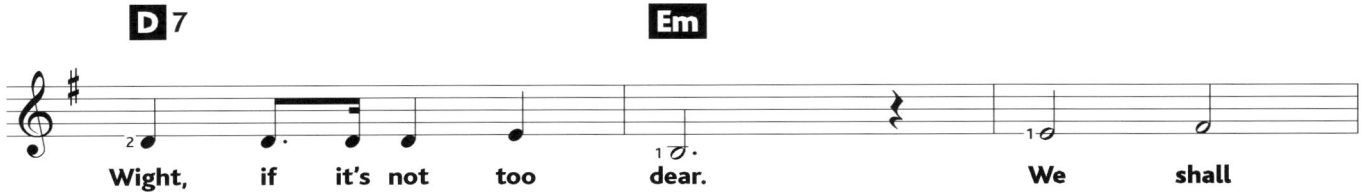
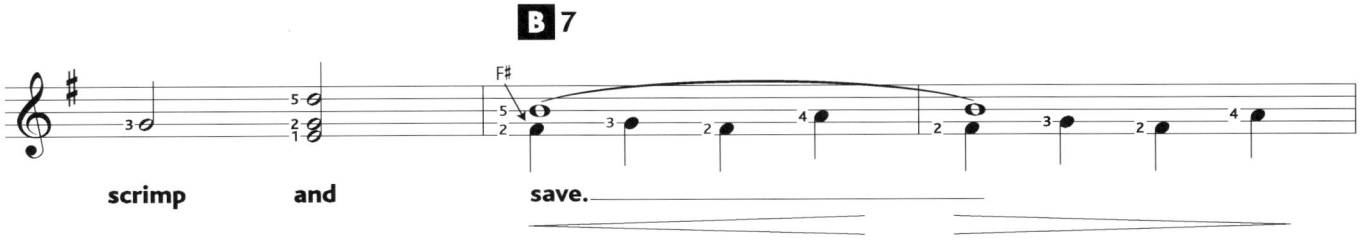
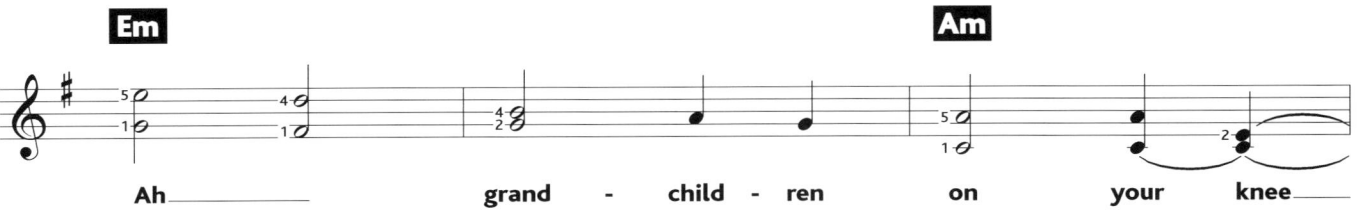

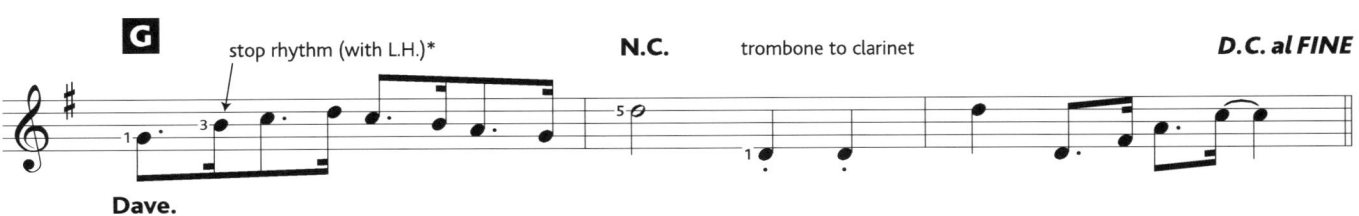

Lesson 6

Chords of G Minor Gm and B♭ Minor B♭m

Using single-finger chord method:

Locate **G** and **B♭** in the accompaniment section of your keyboard.

Convert these notes into Gm and B♭m respectively (see Book 2 and your owner's manual).

Using fingered chord method:

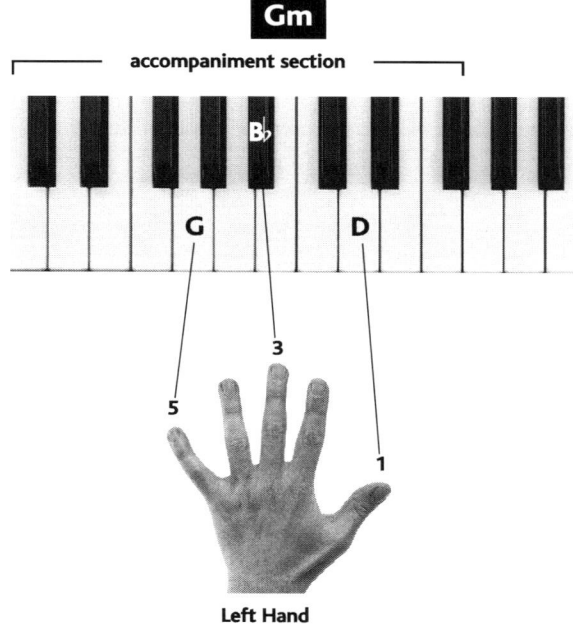

Left Hand

Compare this chord with G major, a chord you already know.

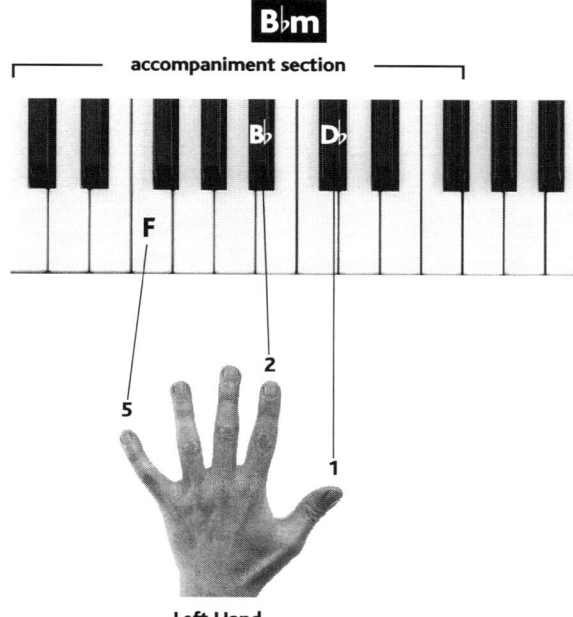

Left Hand

Compare this chord with B♭ major, a chord you already know.
The minor version tends to sound more 'sad' or 'melancholy' but can also be more interesting.

Isn't She Lovely

Words & Music by Stevie Wonder

Stevie Wonder

Voice: **piano, with sustain**
Rhythm: **swing**
Tempo: **medium** (♩ = 115)
Synchro-start: **on**

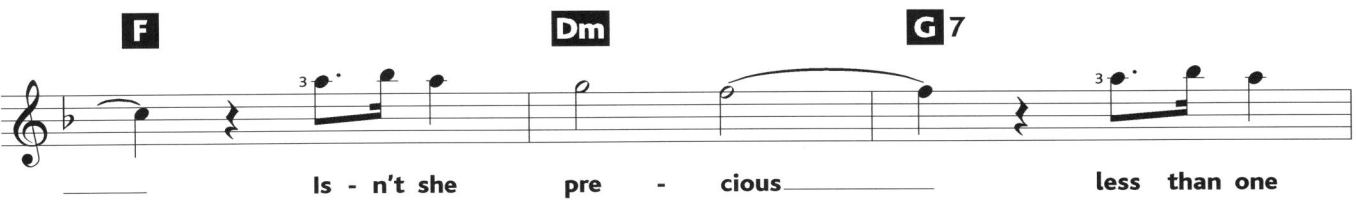

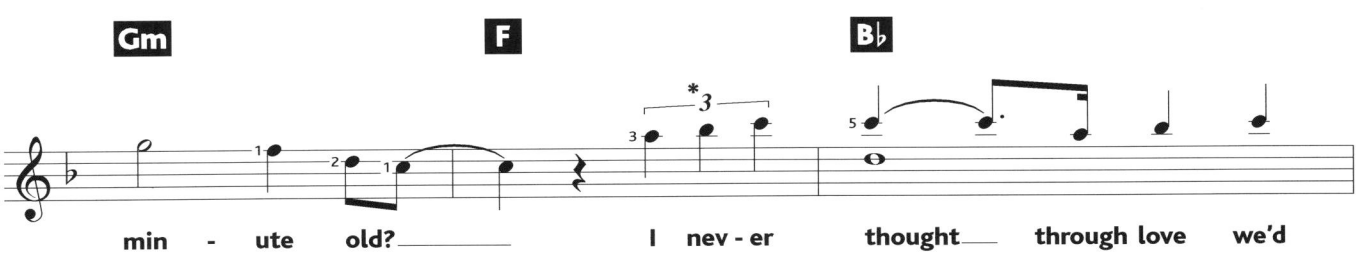

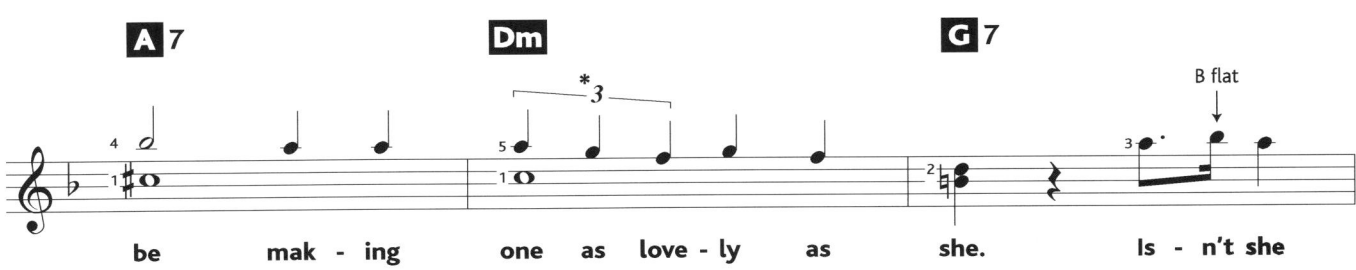

*Quarter note (crotchet) triplet: 3 quarter notes played in the time of 2.
Play these quarter notes slightly faster than usual, in order to fit them into the bar, but keep them even, and equal to each other.

© Copyright 1976 Jobete Music Company Incorporated and Black Bull Music, USA. Jobete Music (UK) Limited/Black Bull Music for the UK & Eire.
All Rights Reserved. International Copyright Secured.

(Everything I Do) I Do It For You

Words by Bryan Adams & Robert John Lange | Music by Michael Kamen

Bryan Adams

Voice: **piano**
Rhythm: **slow rock**
Tempo: **slow** (♩ = 84)
Synchro-start: **on**

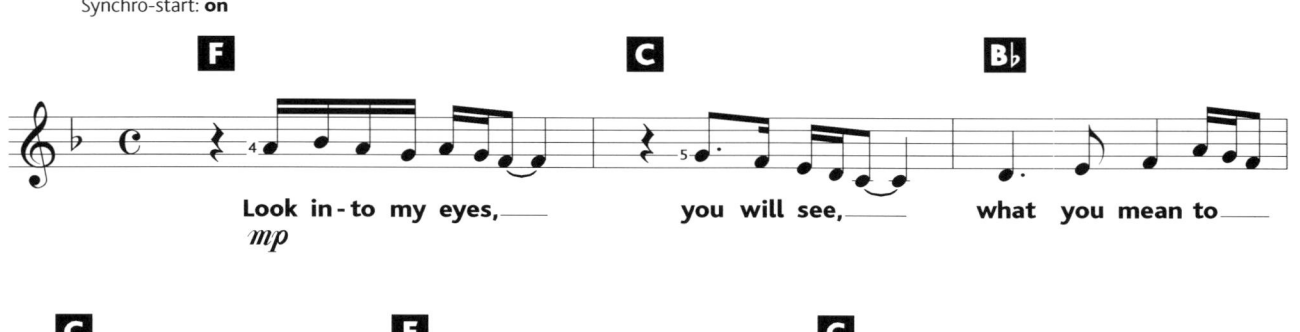
Look in-to my eyes, you will see, what you mean to

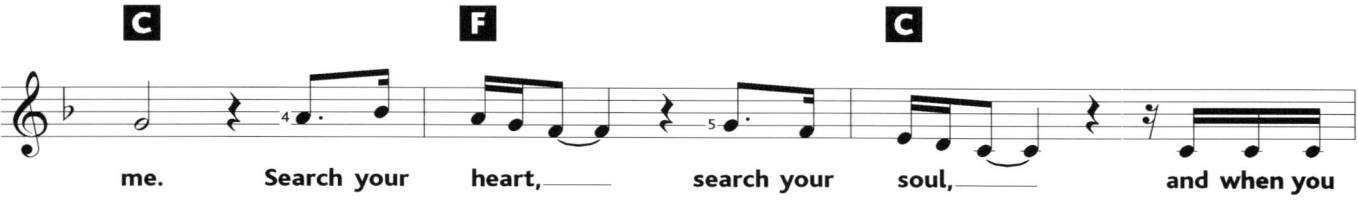
me. Search your heart, search your soul, and when you

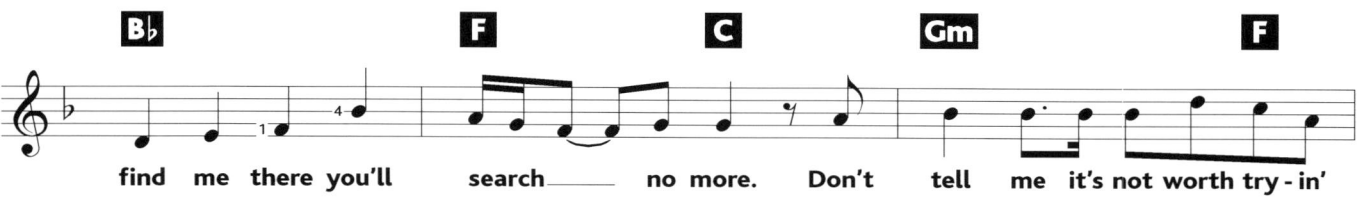
find me there you'll search no more. Don't tell me it's not worth try-in'

for. You can't tell me it's not worth dy-in' for. You know it's

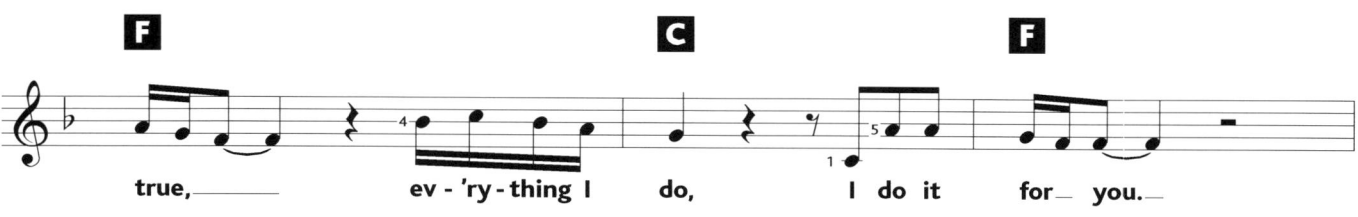
true, ev-'ry-thing I do, I do it for you.

Look in-to your heart, you will find

© Copyright 1991 Universal/MCA Music Limited (62.5%)/ Rondor Music (London) Limited (18.75%)/ Zomba Music Publishers Limited (18.75%).
All Rights Reserved. International Copyright Secured.

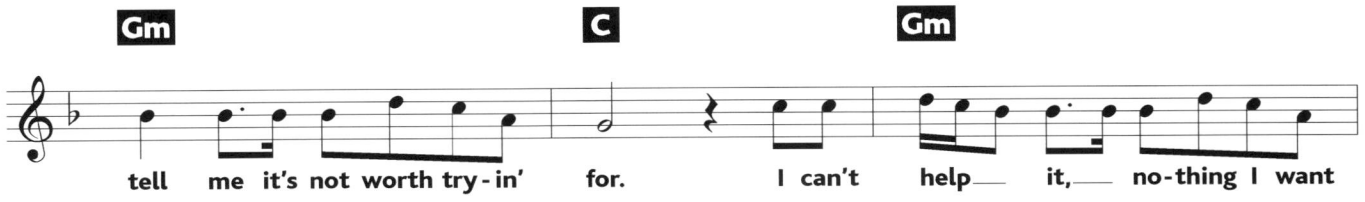

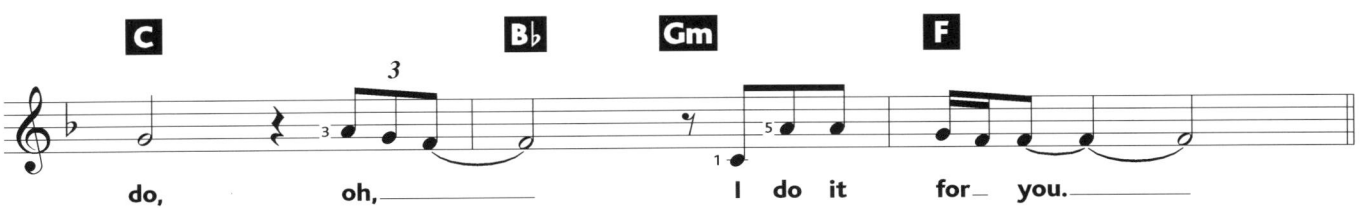

LESSON 7

Minor Keys

So far almost all your playing has been in major keys: C, F and G. Songs written in minor keys, with their abundance of minor chords, often have a sad, nostalgic quality, which makes an excellent contrast.

Key of D Minor

The key of D minor is related to the key of F Major.
The scales on which these keys are built use the same notes:

Scale of D minor ('natural')

D   E   F   G   A   (B♭)   C   D

Scale of F (major)

F   G   A   (B♭)   C   D   E   F

All the notes are white except one: B flat. As you might have guessed, both keys have the same key signature.

Key of D minor

Key of F

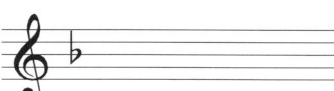

You're probably wondering how to tell the difference between the keys on looking at a piece of music.

Most pieces begin or end on their root note, that is, the note which takes its name from the key.
So a piece in D minor would most probably begin or end on D, and so on.

When playing in the key of D Minor (as in the key of F), you must remember to play all B's, wherever they might appear on the keyboard, as B flats.

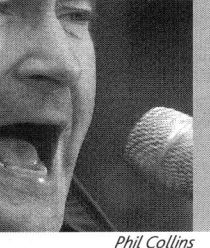

In The Air Tonight

Words & Music by Phil Collins

Phil Collins

Voice: **synth strings**
Rhythm: **dance pop**
Tempo: **medium** (♩= 90)
Synchro-start: **on**

I can feel it com - ing in the air to - night,

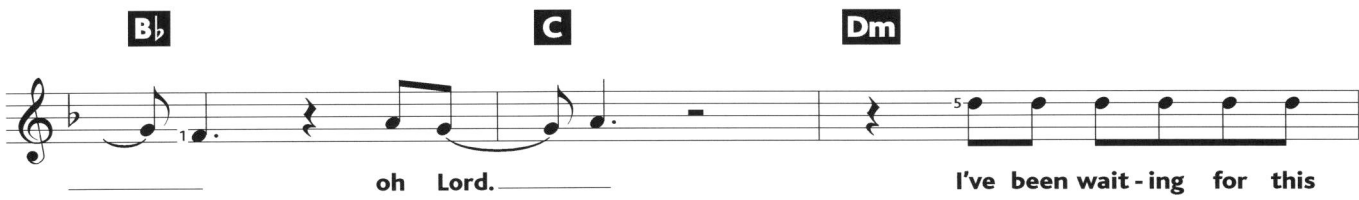

oh Lord. I've been wait - ing for this

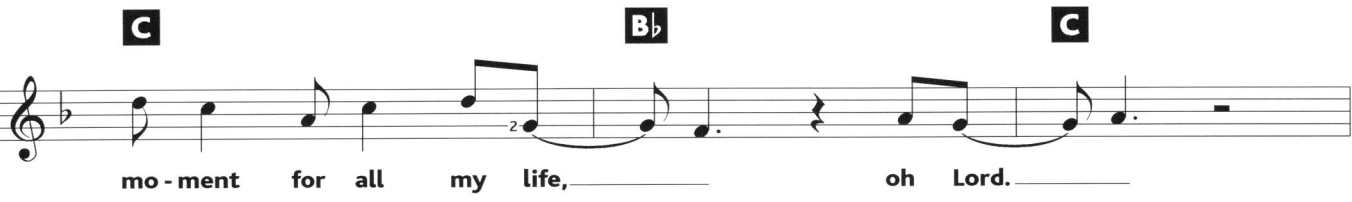

mo - ment for all my life, oh Lord.

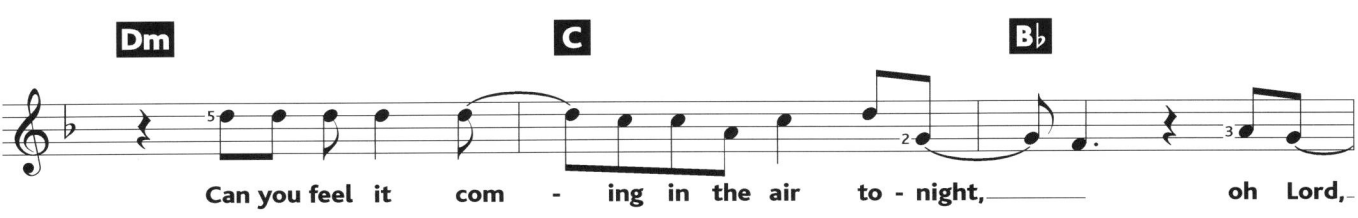

Can you feel it com - ing in the air to - night, oh Lord,

1° hit auto-fill
2° hit end

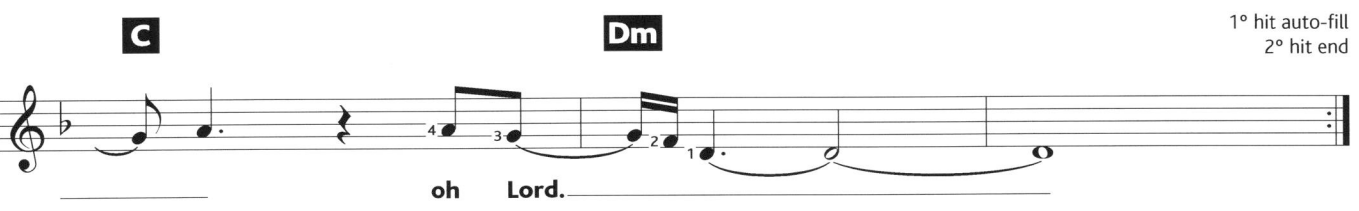

oh Lord.

© Copyright 1981 Effectsound Limited/Hit & Run Music (Publishing) Limited.
All Rights Reserved. International Copyright Secured.

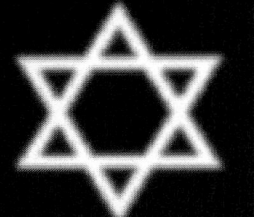

Hava Nagila

Traditional

Voice: **bass clarinet**
Rhythm: **march or swing**
Tempo: **medium** (♩ = 112)
Synchro-start: **on**

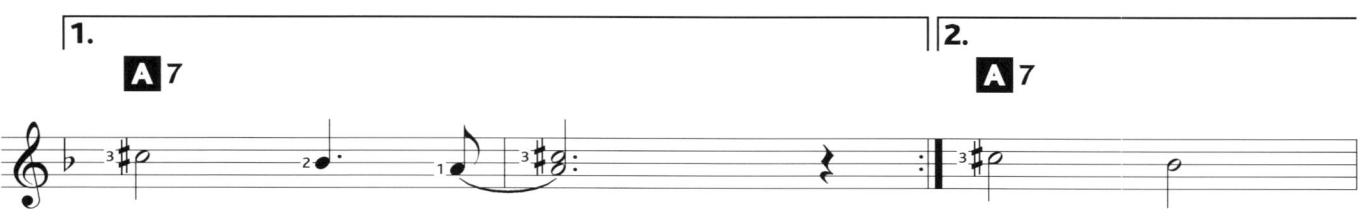

© Copyright 2003 Dorsey Brothers Limited.
All Rights Reserved. International Copyright Secured.

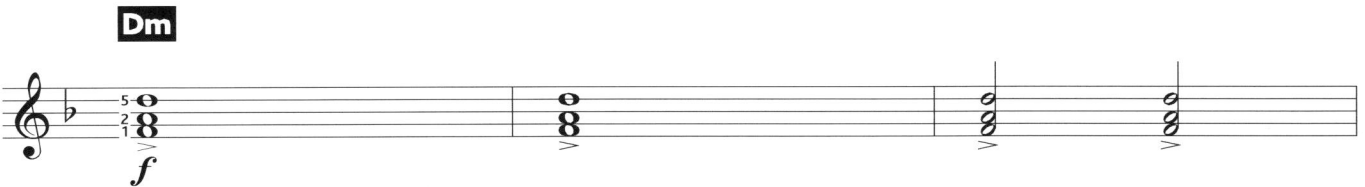
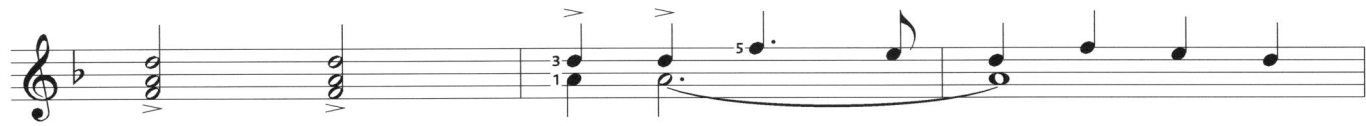
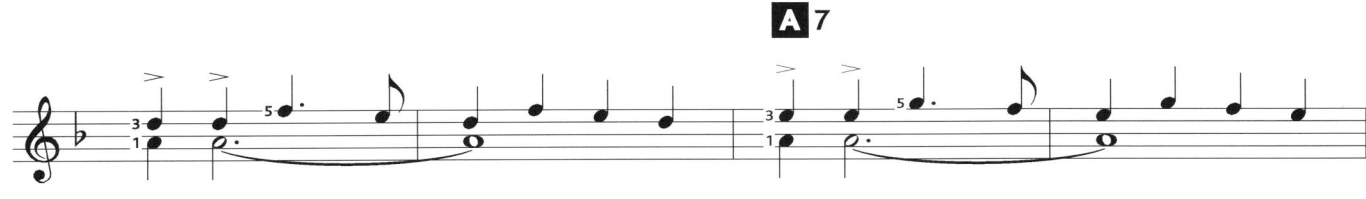
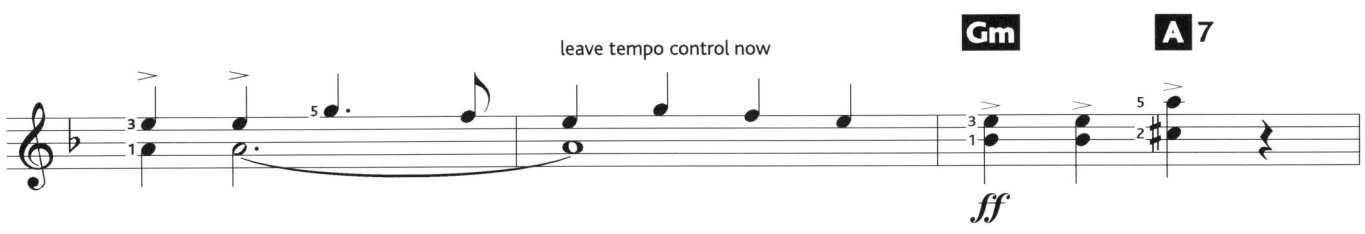

Lesson 8

Key of E Minor

THE KEY OF E MINOR is related to the key of G Major.
Both keys used the same scale notes:

Scale of E minor ('natural')

E F# G A B C D E

Scale of G (major)

G A B C D E F# G

All the notes are white except for F sharp, so the key signature is the same for both keys:

Key of E minor

Key of G
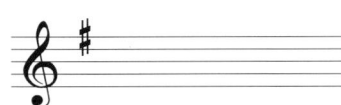

When playing in the key of E Minor (as in the key of G), you must remember to play all F's, wherever they might appear on the keyboard, as F sharps.

Chord of B Minor Bm

Using single-finger chord method:

Locate **B** in the accompaniment section of your keyboard.

Convert this into **Bm** (see Book 2 and your owner's manual). B is the first white note to the left of C.

Using fingered chord method:

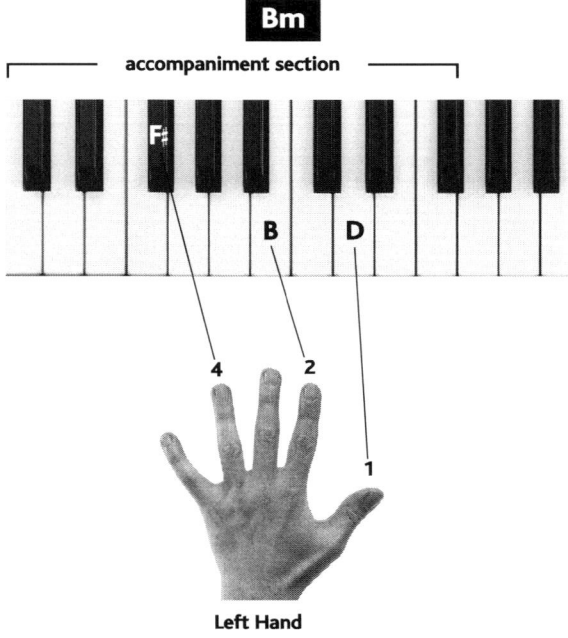

Left Hand

Livin' La Vida Loca

Words & Music by Desmond Child & Robi Rosa

Ricky Martin

Voice: **Brass Ensemble**
Rhythm: **Latin**
Tempo: **fast** (♩= **160**)
Synchro-start: **on**

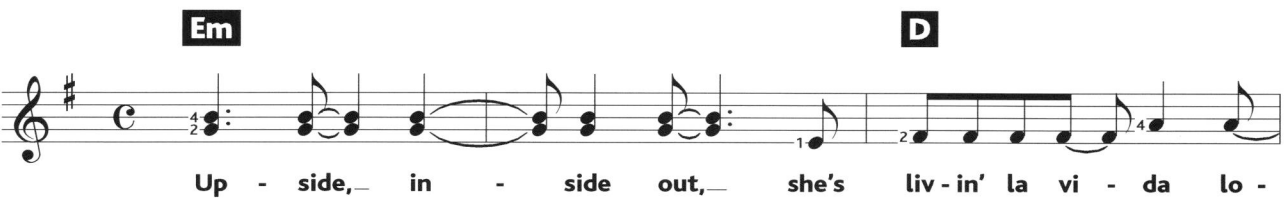

Up - side, in - side out, she's liv - in' la vi - da lo -

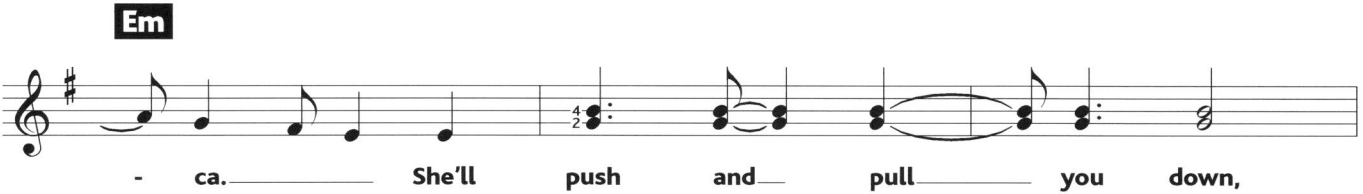

- ca. She'll push and pull you down,

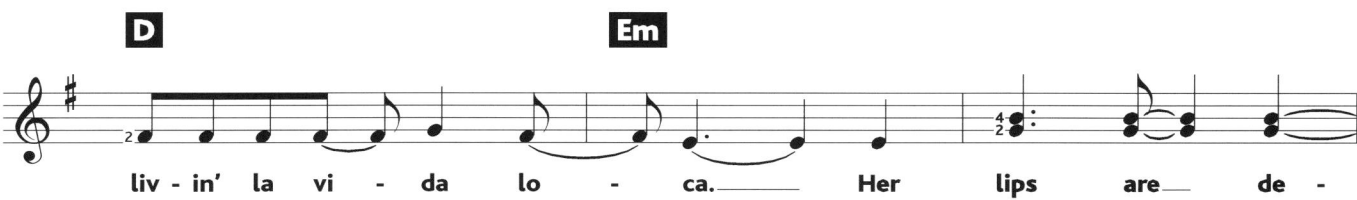

liv - in' la vi - da lo - ca. Her lips are de -

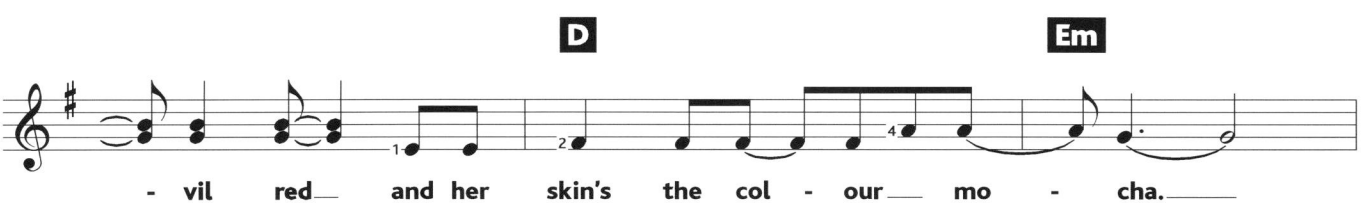

- vil red and her skin's the col - our mo - cha.

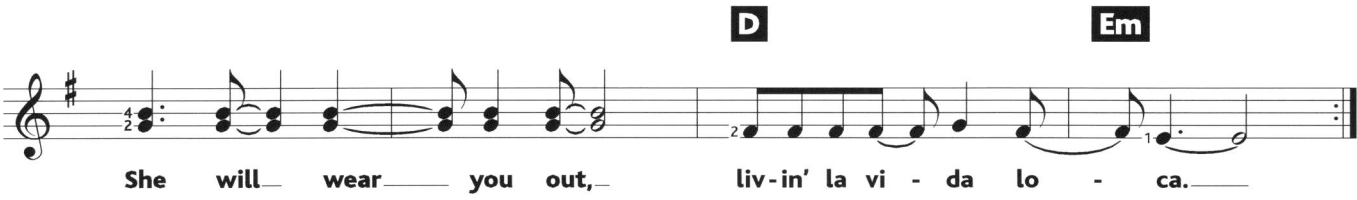

She will wear you out, liv - in' la vi - da lo - ca.

© Copyright 1999 Desmophobia/Universal Music Publishing Limited (50%)/A Phantom Vox Publishing/Muziekuitgeverij Artemis/Warner/Chappell Music Limited (50%).
All Rights Reserved. International Copyright Secured.

The cast of Friends

I'll Be There For You
(Theme from *Friends*)

Words & Music by Michael Skloff, Allee Willis, Philip Solem, David Crane, Marta Kauffman & Danny Wilde

Voice: **guitar**
Rhythm: **8 beat pop**
Tempo: **fast** (♩ = 170)
Synchro-start: **on**

start rhythm here

So no-one told you life was gon-na be this way.

Your job's a joke, you're broke, your

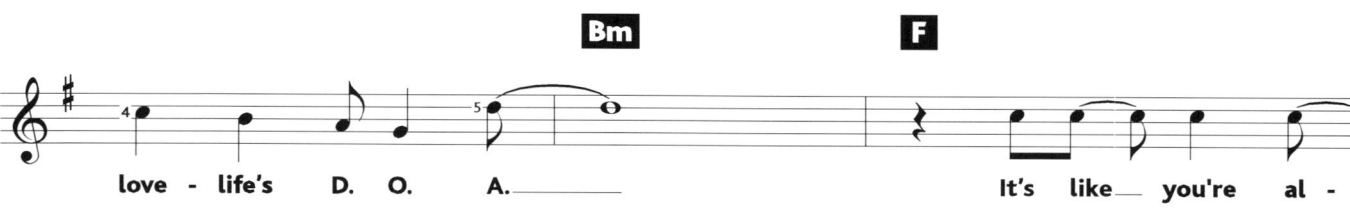

love-life's D. O. A. It's like you're al-

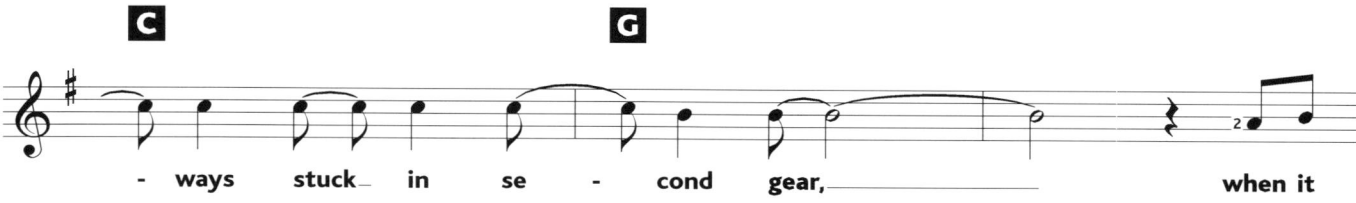

-ways stuck in se-cond gear, when it

© Copyright 1995 Til Dawn Music, USA. Warner/Chappell Music Limited.
All Rights Reserved. International Copyright Secured.

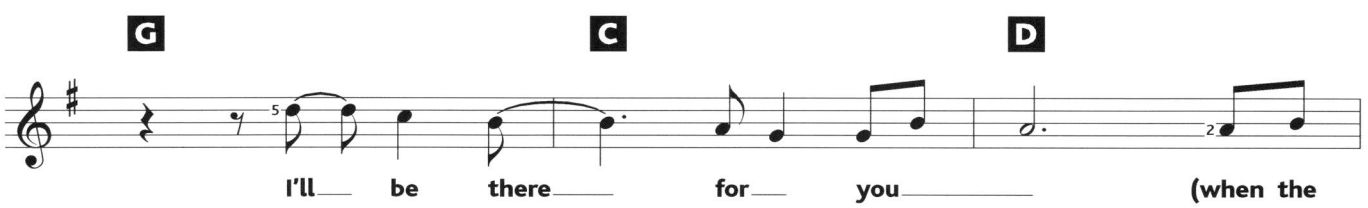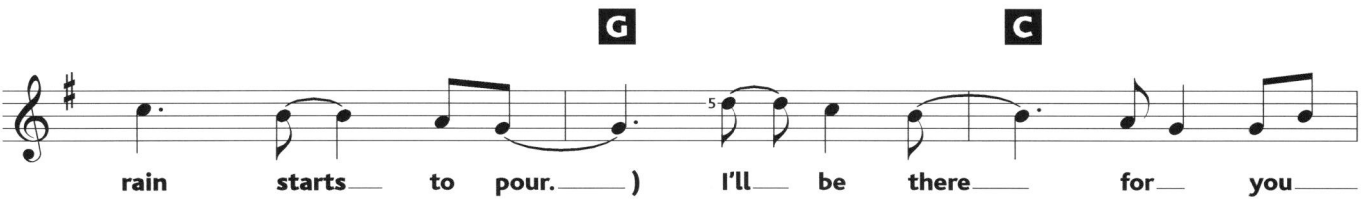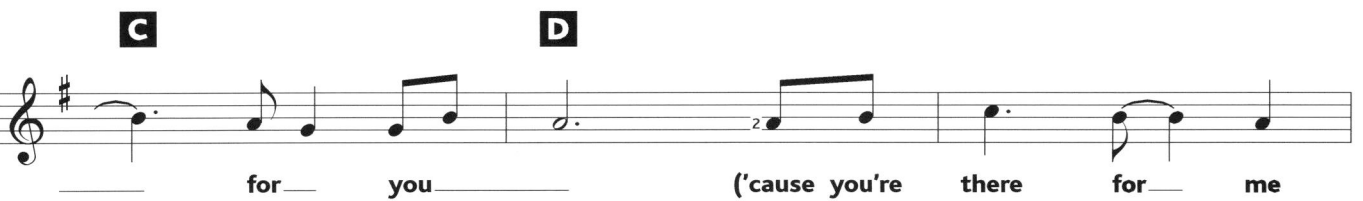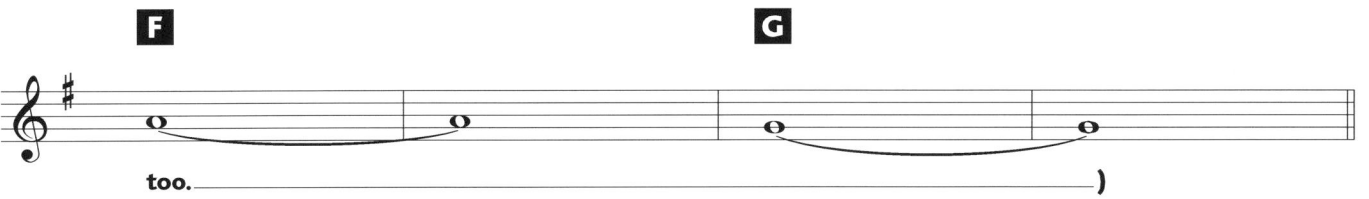

Lesson 9

Key of B Flat

THE SCALE OF B FLAT, and therefore the key of B flat, requires two flats: B flat and E flat:

Scale/Key of B flat (major)

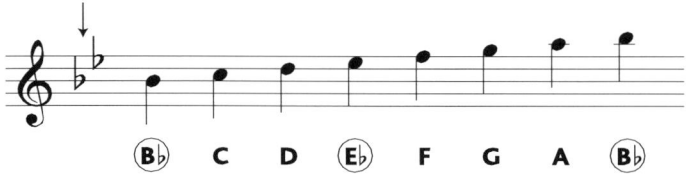

When you are playing in this key you must remember to play all B's and E's, wherever they might fall on the keyboard, as B flats and E flats, respectively.

Chord of E♭

Using single-finger chord method:

Play the note E♭ in the accompaniment section of your keyboard. You can find E♭ by looking to the note to the right of the group of two black notes.

Using fingered chord method:

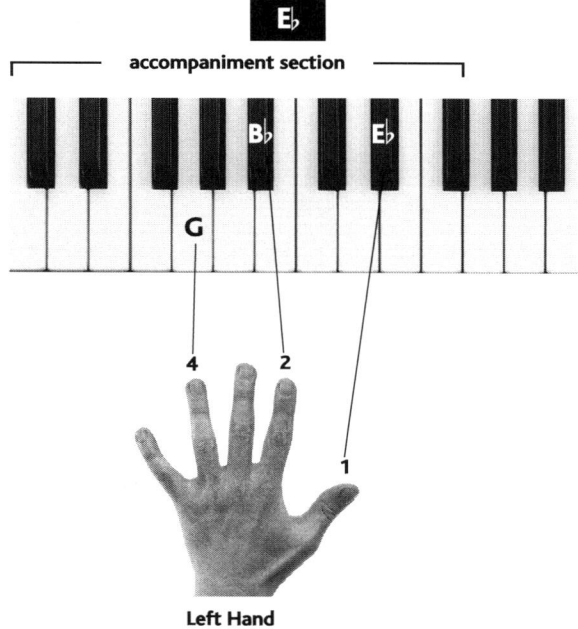

Left Hand

Don't Cry For Me Argentina

Music by Andrew Lloyd Webber | Lyrics by Tim Rice

Madonna

Voice: **trumpet**
Rhythm: **tango**
Tempo: **medium** (♩ = 95)
Synchro-start: **on**

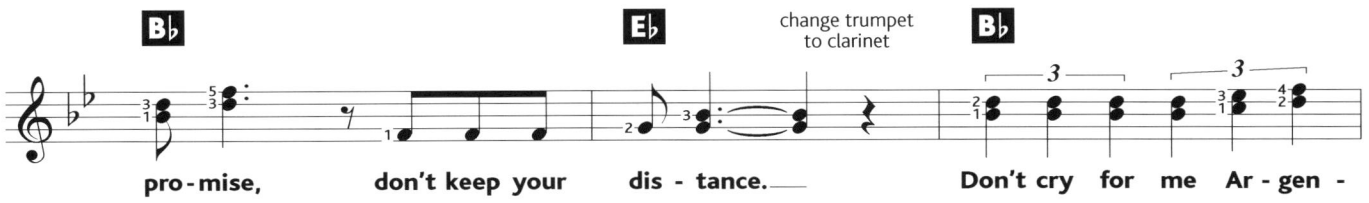

© Copyright 1976 & 1977 Evita Music Limited.
All Rights Reserved. International Copyright Secured.

Mamma Mia

Words & Music by Benny Andersson, Björn Ulvaeus & Stig Anderson

Abba

Voice: **oboe**
Rhythm: **rock**
Tempo: **medium** (♩ = 135)
Synchro-start: **on**

VERSE

I've been cheat-ed by you___ since I don't___ know when.
So I made up my mind___ it must come to an end.

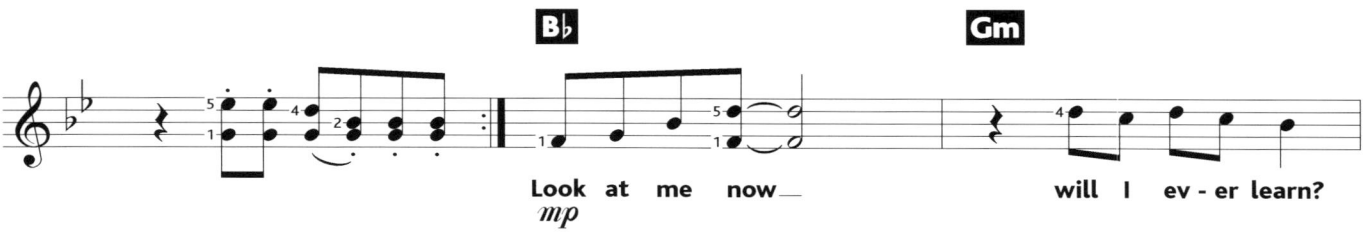

Look at me now___ will I ev-er learn?

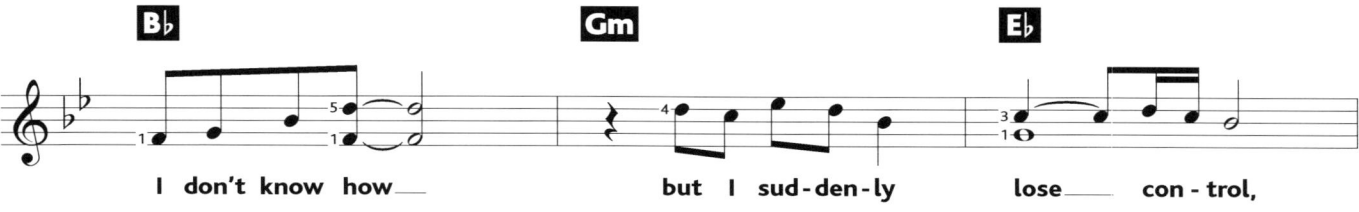

I don't know how___ but I sud-den-ly lose___ con-trol,

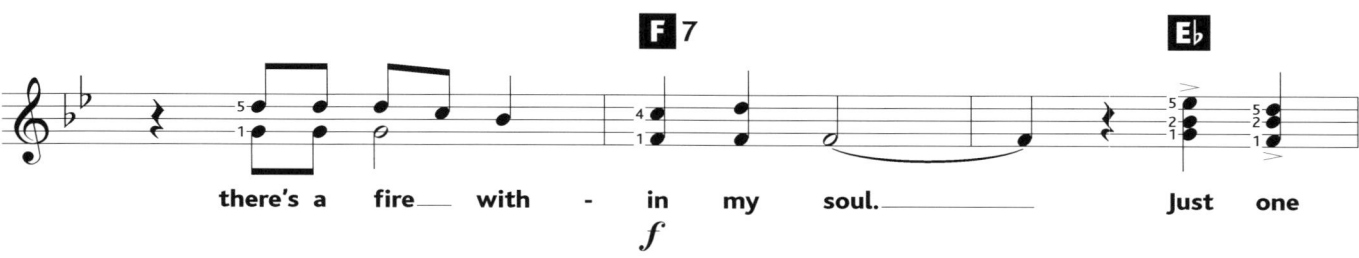

there's a fire___ with - in my soul. Just one

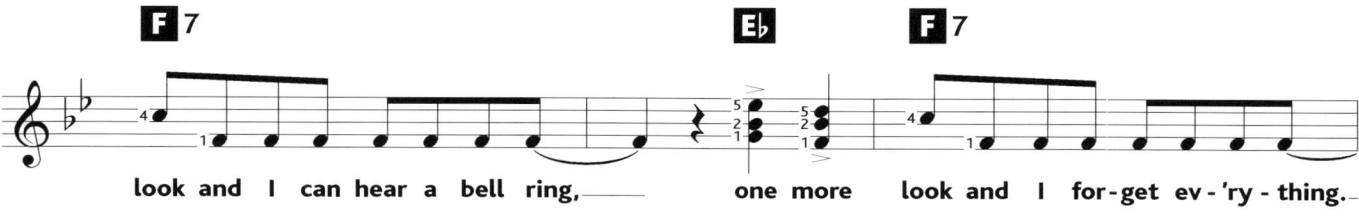

look and I can hear a bell ring,___ one more look and I for-get ev-'ry-thing.

© Copyright 1975 Union Songs AB, Stockholm, Sweden for the world.
Bocu Music Limited for Great Britain and the Republic of Ireland. All Rights Reserved. International Copyright Secured.

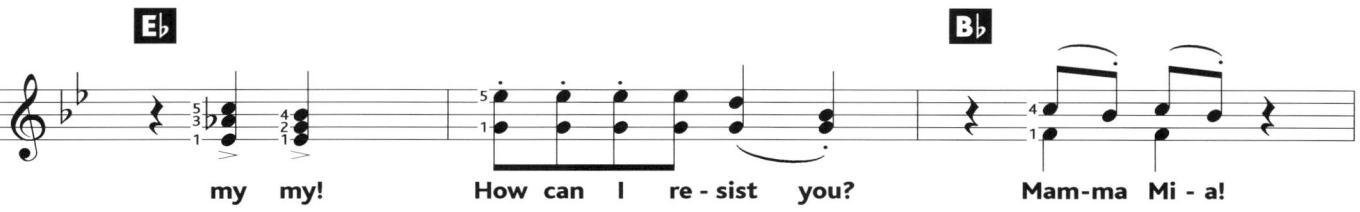

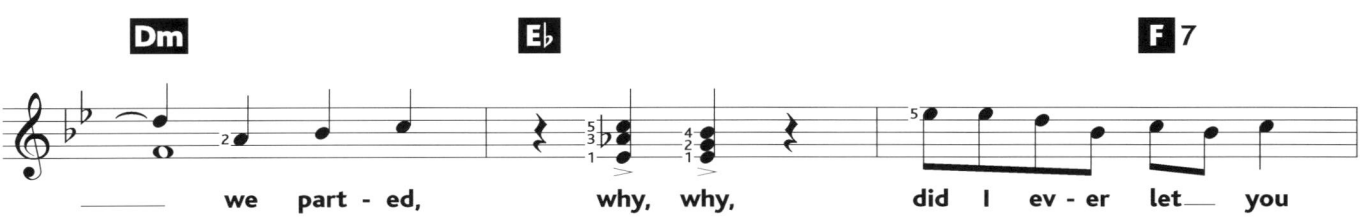
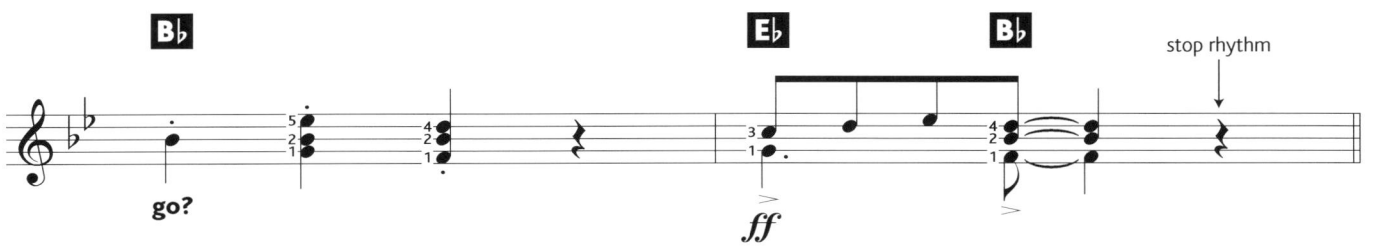

Chord of C Minor Cm

Using single-finger chord method:

Locate **C** in the accompaniment section of your keyboard. Convert this note into **Cm**

(see Book 2, page 30 and your owner's manual).

Using fingered chord method

See diagram (right).

Compare this chord with **C** major, a chord you already know.

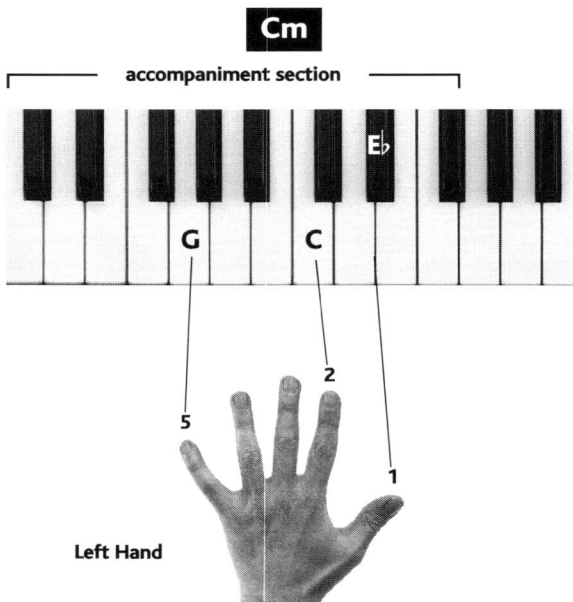

Left Hand

Clocks

Words & Music by Guy Berryman, Jon Buckland, Will Champion & Chris Martin

Coldplay

Voice: **piano**
Rhythm: **8 beat**
Tempo: **medium** (♩ = 125)
Synchro-start: **on**

PIANO INTRO

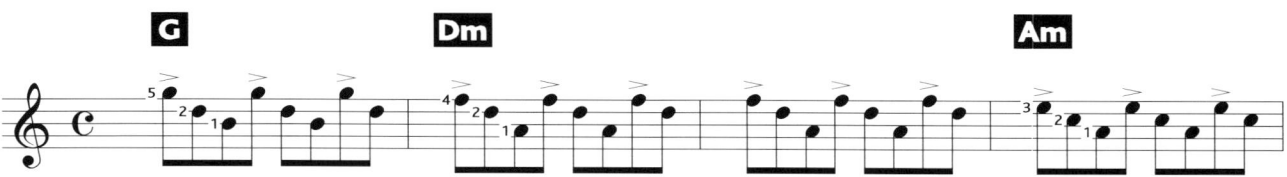

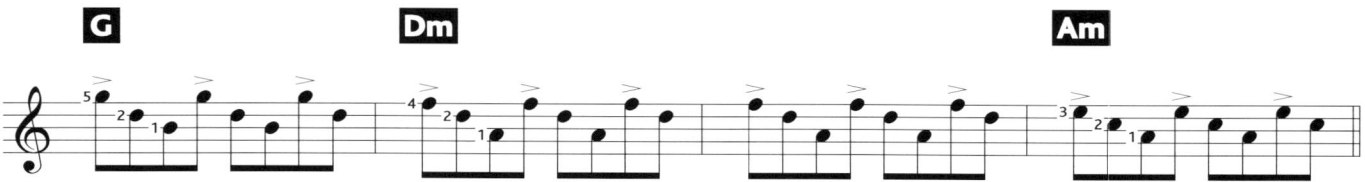

VERSE

Lights go out and I can't be saved, tides that I tried to

© Copyright 2002 BMG Music Publishing Limited.
All Rights Reserved. International Copyright Secured.

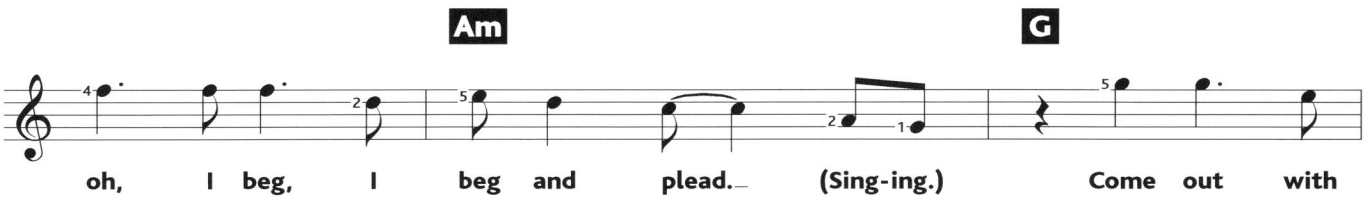
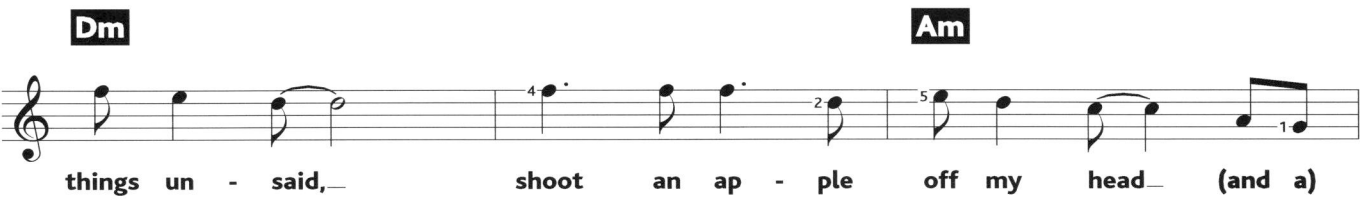

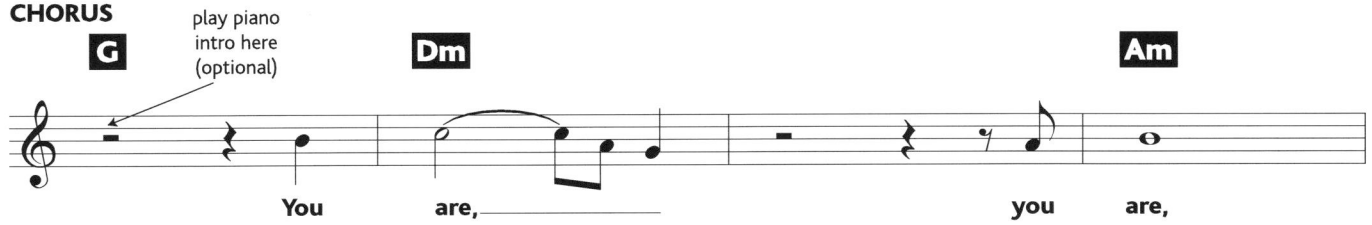

Star Wars (Main Theme)

By John Williams

Harrison Ford

Voice: **brass or orchestral ensemble**
Rhythm: **march**
Tempo: **medium** (♩ = 108)
Synchro-start: **on**

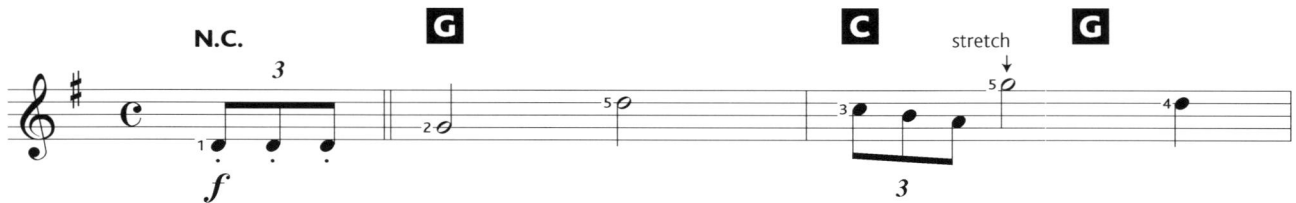
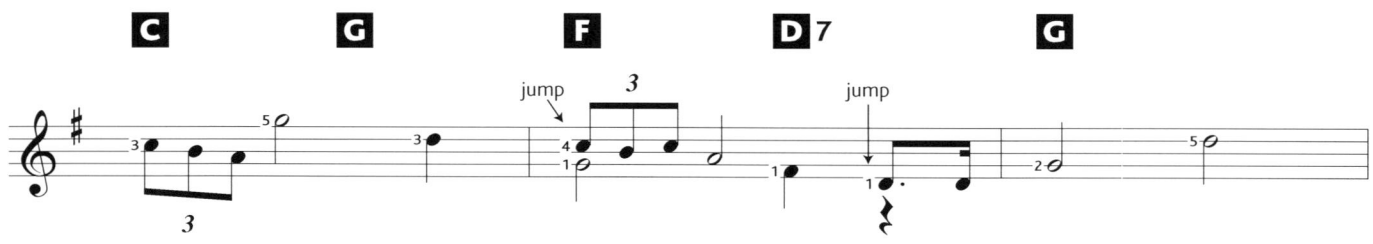
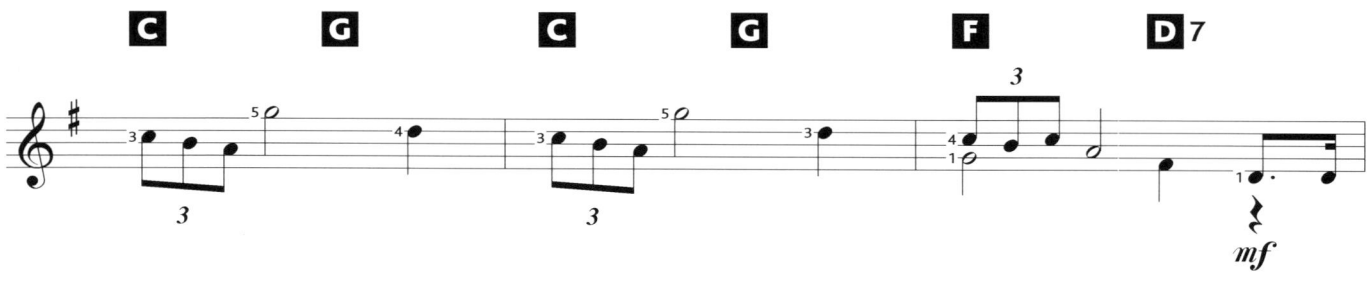
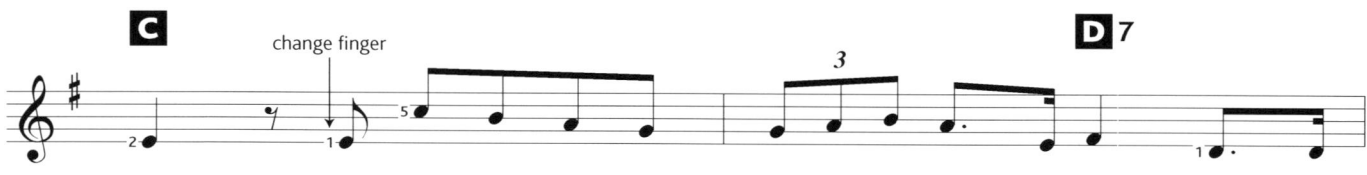
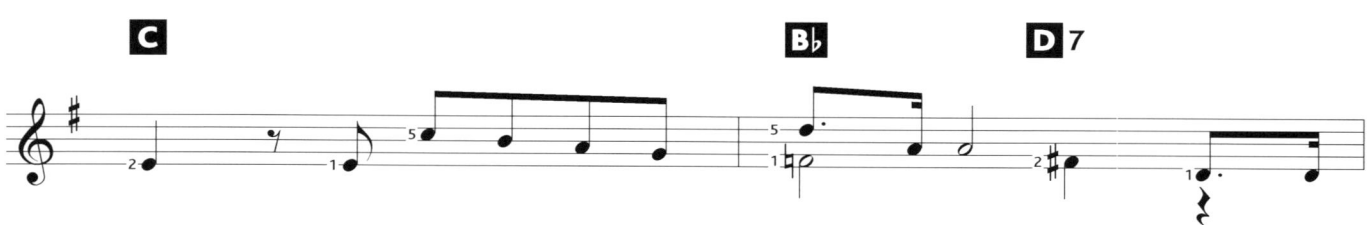

© Copyright 1977 Fox Fanfare Music Incorporated & Bantha Music, USA.
Warner Chappell Music Limited. All Rights Reserved. International Copyright Secured.

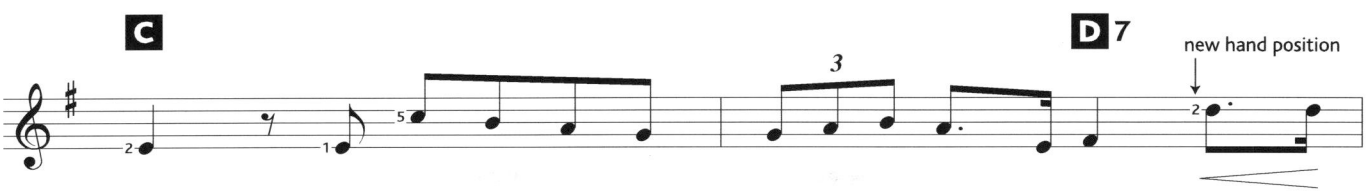
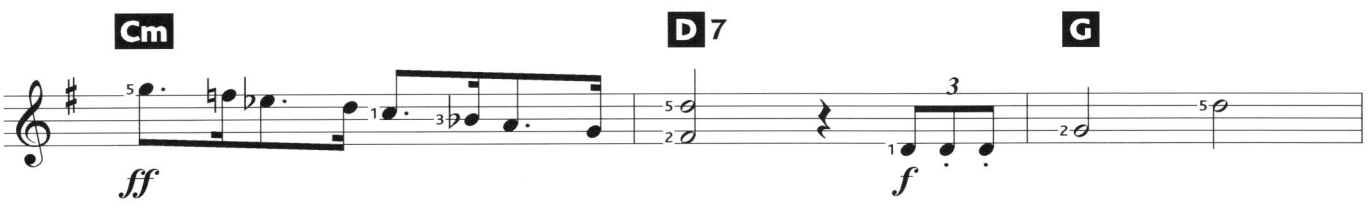
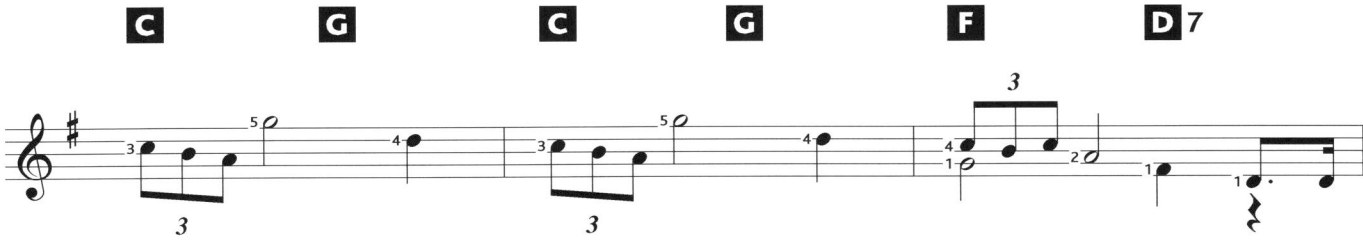
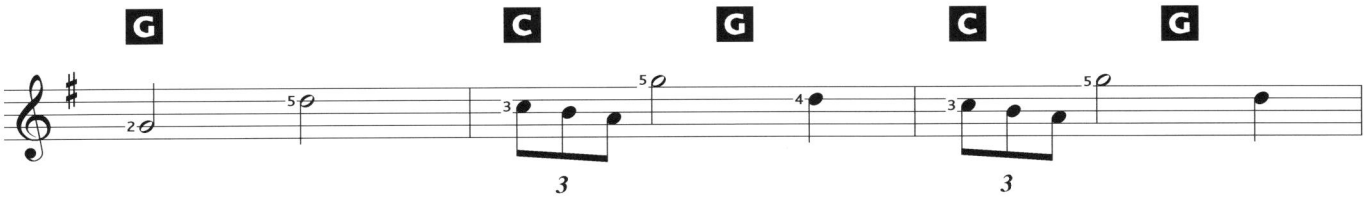
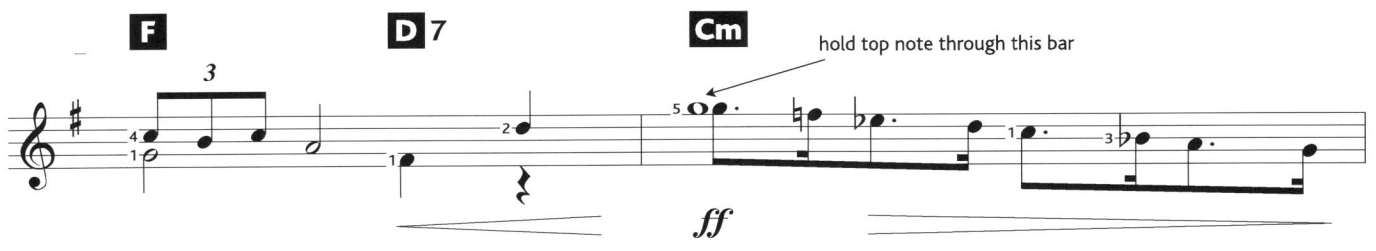

Congratulations...

ON COMPLETING **Book 3** of *The Complete Keyboard Player*!

You have achieved a good standard of playing, and now need to expand your repertoire with more great songs. Why not check out *The Complete Keyboard Player* repertoire books, available from all good music shops.

Chord Chart

Showing all 'fingered' chords used in the course so far:

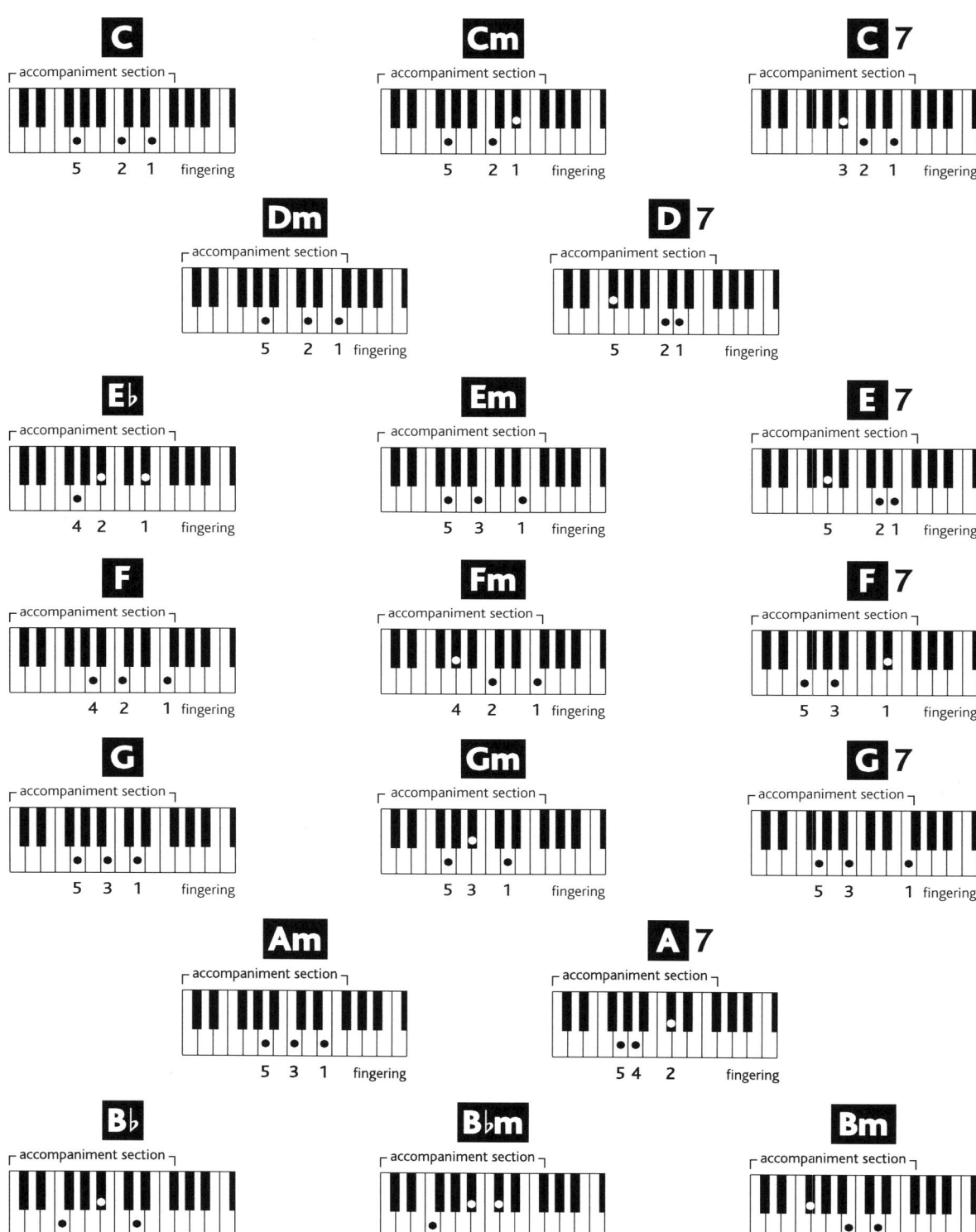